The Gentle Self

How to Overcome Your Difficulties with Depression, Anxiety, Shyness and Low Self-esteem

By Gerti Schoen

D0104609

Contents

1. The Gentle Self

All my life I was shy. I didn't always know it. In fact, it was in some ways easier as long as I wasn't aware of it. It was quite a revelation when I started opening my eyes to it. But one after another the blinders came down, slowly but surely, and I had to deal with the social anxiety, the withdrawal, the feelings of being on the outside looking in, the sense that I wasn't sure where to belong. I had to confront the loss of so many friends in the past because I hadn't learned where to draw the line and how to work things out. Nobody had taught me.

But things changed. It was not an easy ride. Still gets bumpy at times. But it was quite radical in the way things took a turn for the better. It's all about creating awareness. My husband used to tease me: "Are you in your head again? You have to look out!" He doesn't have to remind me of that any more. Not often, anyway.

I remember a mild March day, spring was already in the air. I walked home from my work as a psychotherapist, feeling blessed for having such a meaningful profession, where I can have an impact on others and identify with my clients. Often I know exactly what they are going through, having already made it well into the journey they have just embarked upon.

I have struggled with the same fears of feeling inadequate, thinking I have nothing to say and that I would forever be the outsider from some elusive circle I wanted to get into, or from a well-functioning family I felt like I didn´t belong to.

That evening, I was smiling about an encounter I had just had with a young man whose round face still bore the features of a boy. He struggled with identifying his own beliefs against an unending tide of other people´s opinions, feeling overpowered by their convictions, not knowing after a while what his own point of view even was.

I´ve been in this place before. Many times. Nowadays, it doesn't happen so much anymore. I've gotten to know myself. I know when to stand up for what I believe in and when to go with the flow. When to override my instinct to withdraw and when to keep ploughing ahead instead. Sometimes I don't have an opinion. I can see both sides, several sides. I can´t say for sure that this person is right and that one is wrong. I am better able to tolerate not knowing what "the truth" of that moment is, because there are many truths, many perspectives, and the currents eventually rejoin the river, sometimes happily, sometimes after great struggle.

Most of the time the old issues aren´t issues any more, because I learned that I do much better in small, quiet settings than in big gatherings. I don´t care to go to crowded bars and loud parties anymore. I don´t like them. I don´t miss the disconnect, the waning attention spans, the escapism. I prefer forming my own social circles according to my own preferences. There are still days when the old patterns emerge, but I don't mind so much any more. I know why I do what I do and I can cut myself some slack. There´ll be other days when I can make up for it.

While I consider myself a gentle self, I don´t identify so strongly with all the negative traits of this personality type any more. Maybe it´s just because I don´t take myself as seriously as I used to. There´s nothing wrong really. Except on days when there is.

2. What Is Narcissism?

The personality of the gentle self has a lot to do with narcissism. Here's how. Narcissism has many faces. It is usually associated with people who are considered "selfish" or only talk about themselves without paying any attention to others. We think of television characters like the greedy and reckless JR from the TV series *Dallas* or a more modern version, the sex-obsessed Edie of *Desperate Housewives*. Narcissism has often been used to characterize a particularly bad relationship, when a self-centered man or woman has nothing but his or her own interests in mind. In the age of live competitions like *American Idol* and reality-TV shows like *Survivor*, we think about young adults who want to be famous and showered in adoration without bothering much about the responsibilities daily life holds. We believe narcissism is about the grandiose fantasies of an immature mind that focuses solely on fame, perfection and simply on being either "the best" or on finding the perfect mate in whose glory they can shine. Sometimes people fall victim to a narcissist, be it a partner or a parent, who has no capacity to consider their points of view, and thus the victim's personality is obliterated by that domineering persona who can barely tolerate even the slightest attention being paid to others.

But there is a flip side to that single-minded picture of narcissism that has been taken over by the mainstream. Narcissism is not only at play in people who need to showcase their ego to the extreme. It is just as prevalent in *those who constantly do away with their needs* and put others first at all times while depleting their own resources and neglecting their own points of view. It is those of us who can´t ever say no to other people´s demands and feel too fragile to stand up for themselves. Their sense of self is such that they feel predominantly inferior to others, and this vulnerable self sometimes remains altogether undefined. They don´t know who they are and what they want and how to get what they need. Their narcissistic needs have been oppressed and destroyed by other people´s agendas, and they feel they have no choice but to continue to suppress their own instincts and desires. They become fragile and withdrawn, and many are introverts who look inside for solutions rather than for help from the outside world.

Narcissism basically means that one´s sense of self is out of balance, that there is either too little of us or too much of us, which puts others off either way and makes equal relationships difficult. In many narcissistic relationships, one partner will always have the upper hand and the weaker partner will either suffer from chronic depression or will walk away in pursuit of a relationship that promises to be more fulfilling, which often turns out to be equally dissatisfying. What´s lacking is a genuine ability to engage with the other, to connect on an equal, deeper level, and an environment that feels safe enough to disagree with the other without losing face or the whole relationship.

Because many people who chronically suppress their own needs come across as gentle and accommodating to others, they are exclusively seen as "nice guys" or "sweet girls" who can easily be asked a favor or made friends with. What often happens is that the favors that are being asked of them become too much, and carrying the burden of maintaining a friendship turns one-sided. Because the "nice guy" has never learned how to ask for having his own needs met, he has no other choice but to walk away and lose another relationship in the process.

To children of narcissistic parents it often comes as a shock to recognize stark similarities between their own narcissistic self-preoccupation and that of the parent. Where the classical narcissist complains loudly about being neglected and demands attention, the "gentle narcissist" craves the same but remains withdrawn into his own mind. Where the former can´t stop talking about herself in the most glowing tones, the latter can´t cease to think in the most self-critical ways. Both are constantly wondering about how they come across to others, what they did right or — more likely — wrong, fully absorbed in their relentless thinking about themselves.

I call the representatives of the more agreeable version of the two kinds of narcissism "gentle narcissist," or alternatively the "gentle self": many of us are shy and withdrawn or suffer from anxiety, depression and low self-esteem. Some are quite sociable, but their relationships remain shallow and devoid of intimacy and are always at risk of falling apart. What the two types of narcissism have in common is a certain softness and fragility in personality, a gentleness which tends to make it hard to face relationships head on. As soon as the imbalance between their own needs and those of others gets out of hand, they become withdrawn and lonely and have a hard time dealing with their environment, which is often experienced as overly aggressive and uncaring. The main way they cope with their insecurities and their vulnerable selves is by withdrawing from the world, which cuts them off from the most basic sources of self-esteem and well-being: relationships. In their heart of hearts, they crave nothing more than to be more involved with the world and other people, but they cannot bring themselves to overcome a certain paralysis and fear of rejection and remain on the outskirts of life, never quite able to express themselves fully and to verbalize their frustrations openly.

I have derived the terms "gentle narcissist" and "gentle self" from the work of the American self-psychologist Heinz Kohut, whose groundbreaking work on the structure of the self and on narcissism has never received the attention outside of psychoanalytic circles that it deserves. In this book, I will explain how gentle narcissists' inner lives are organized, why so many feel compelled to retreat from the world, how to form fulfilling relationships, and how to get back on track to live a fuller and happier life.

Many people dread being called narcissistic, mostly because narcissists have a reputation for being self-absorbed and vain. Unlike many of their well-known siblings, the self-involved and attention demanding classical narcissists, gentle narcissists are quite able to form meaningful relationships once they feel safe enough to come out of their shells and begin to trust a world that they have experienced as overwhelming and insensitive. They do have a genuine capacity to connect but are forced to use defenses like avoidance, non-commitment and emotional distance out of fear that their weakened self will be taken over too easily, and ultimately because they are terrified of losing or being rejected by the people they have learned to trust. Beneath their sometimes aloof and standoffish behavior, they very much crave connection with others.

Paradoxically, no proper clinical diagnosis for the gentle narcissist exists in the medical world, and their mental health charts often contain simple diagnostic terms like "depression," "anxiety" or "Personality Disorder, Not Otherwise Specified." They often display a prominent anxiety from which they may try to distract themselves by being overly clean and organized or by overeating or picking at their bodies; thus they sometimes are diagnosed with "Obsessive Compulsive Disorder." Other times they are told they suffer from "Adult Attention Deficit Disorder," which stems from their tendency to be pulled in a million directions at once and being unable to make decisions. Some are even thrown into the category of Bipolar Disorders, which occurs when they are easily overwhelmed and fall into a frenzy, a pattern that is nowadays quickly diagnosed as hypomania.

Only very recently, this personality style was finally included in a new textbook called the *Psychodynamic Diagnostic Manual*, published by a number of international psychoanalytic associations. Unfortunately, even here it is summed up in just four lines. The gentle narcissist is here classified as "Narcissistic Personality Disorder: Depressed/Depleted" as opposed to the classic "Arrogant/Entitled" narcissist. Indeed, many gentle narcissists who seek psychotherapeutic treatment are depressed, lack energy and feel depleted by what they have had to endure in their individual lives. A large part of their life force has been suppressed and squeezed out of them, and they are longing for a new life that provides more energy, passion and joy.

As with every psycho-emotional style, this personality type covers a very wide continuum: in the severest form of this kind of narcissism, and on gentle narcissists' worst days, they feel chronically depleted and depressed and are unable to cope with the world. They feel so vulnerable that every human contact is unconsciously experienced as a threat to their well-being, and the only thing they feel capable of is to withdraw or sleep. On these days they might even cut out other people who care about them. At other times they might feel uncomfortable and empty and in need of a supportive listener, and when they get what they need they go about their normal business all day without being impacted much by any kind of stress. It all depends on their individual histories and relationships.

The key to change and a happier life is to become aware: of our needs, of what we are saying and what we are doing and how this affects others.

Once we know what we need, it is important to have the support to go through with it. *Awareness* and *support* are the two columns for change for the gentle narcissist. When they are in place, it is a lot easier to battle the mountain of negative beliefs we tend to have about ourselves. One of the hardest tasks is to quiet the endless critical voices in our heads that convince us all too easily that "something is wrong with me," "I am a burden to others" or "I am worthless" and the many variations of self-loathing. Once we can truly understand that many of these beliefs are mostly in our heads and usually have nothing to do with reality, the grip they have on us fades away and we can focus simply on what the present moment has to offer without having it spoiled by all these negative convictions.

We all know the story of Narcissus, who fell in love with his own mirror image in the water and drowned while adoring himself. It is a tragic and beautiful metaphor for our unending self-involvement, which takes up most of our energy and leaves little room to genuinely think about others. Gentle narcissists too are involved in an endless spiral of self-centered thoughts — even though, sadly, these thoughts usually focus on what we think is wrong with us. The journey is to start looking in the mirror and to begin noticing what is beautiful about us and to take pride in what we have to offer. Only by regarding our own needs can we truly begin to give to others.

3. Going Back to the Roots

The most prevalent difficulty many gentle narcissists have is that of missing out on a certain engagement with the world: either they feel that they are too shy or aloof to really be themselves around others, or their relationships remain on the surface without real intimacy. Withdrawal becomes part of the problem. Withdrawing from a world that seems harsh and hostile is the most dominant characteristic of the gentle narcissist. By withdrawing we continue a behavioral pattern that is most likely formed when we are little.

The pattern begins early: Research on infants, for example, has shown that toddlers spontaneously fall asleep when they feel overwhelmed. Who hasn't observed one of those overburdened parents on the subway or in the street who yells at the child in distress, while the only reaction the child has left is to turn away or stand in frozen terror. Other babies are simply neglected by mothers who ignore their crying repeatedly. They become frustrated and try to pick up the volume, and if that doesn't do the trick, they will eventually just give up. If a repair of what the child experiences as an emotional shock and rejection doesn't occur, if the parent does not pick the child up and soothes his fear and frustration but leaves him to his own undeveloped devices, he will inevitably learn to withdraw from these overwhelming situations, especially if this happens over and over again and there is no one else who can compensate for the repeated failure to comfort the child.

The message the child hears is, *I am not really welcome here, so I'll just make myself smaller or invisible. If I can make myself not want anything and need as little as possible, then I don't have to endure any more frustration.* Later in life, the capacity to pay attention to other people's needs and to have a sense of responsibility for others is diminished because the person feels fragile and unsupported and believes that she has nothing of value to give. The outcome is habitual turning away, escaping, distancing, becoming unavailable to others — a pattern we observe so often in our friends and loved ones. The neglected child thus becomes an adult who is cautious of others and frequently falls back on his own inner world, which feels safer and easier to control but at the same time is empty and disconnected.

Not everyone who experiences such failures in the way our parents raised us turns into a hermit. Depending on your parents' personalities, your genes and the influences of other important people in your upbringing and throughout your life, it can go the opposite way. Maybe someone in your immediate environment, an aunt or a grandparent, was positive and encouraged you to express yourself. Some of us may feel inspired to engage in an artistic field: write novels, create art, act, or sing. We crave positive feedback and seek a means to express ourselves without running into someone else's opposition or resistance or jealousy of what we have to show. Although an audience can always boo and a critic can write a bad review, at least those people aren't immediately present and we don't have to deal with their criticism and the dreaded confrontation directly. The need to retreat is far greater when the injury has been inflicted by someone we wanted to trust but came back to hurt us than when it's coming from an anonymous person.

Behavioral patterns often have to do with the convictions we gained about ourselves as children. If you feel undeserving of an admired person's attention, like that of a parent or a teacher, or that you have to thank someone a thousand times for doing you a small favor, then your caregivers somehow very early on communicated to you that you couldn't expect to get their attention, or that it was not to be taken for granted that you deserve to be cared for. That doesn't necessarily mean that your parents didn't actually care about you. They might have made a sincere attempt at providing a nurturing environment but may not have had the financial or emotional capacities to become a supportive parent. Maybe they had no choice but to spend all their energy on a seriously ill family member, or they were depressed and anxiety-ridden because of their own insecurities and unfulfilled desires.

But because children—and many times adults—have no concept of relational and circumstantial factors and always fall back on their own developmentally appropriate, self-centered perspective, they inevitably end up feeling rejected and not really loved and build convictions like *I am a burden, It is all my responsibility,* or *I am not lovable; something is wrong with me.* Unfortunately, these beliefs tend to hang around for a long time. We may or may not be aware of them, but they influence our daily lives and our relationships. The inevitable consequence of having those particular underlying convictions in our heads is withdrawal.

Intrusion is another reason why retreating becomes necessary . A parent who finds meaning only in her unending love for her child ends up constantly invading the child's personal space. Smothering the child with what becomes too much attention and not leaving her any room to decide for herself about how to engage with the other will also result in withdrawal. The child experiences the constant interest in her physical appearance or emotional process as intrusive, over-stimulating and overwhelming and has no other choice but to disengage.

The same thing happens when an overly self-interested parent constantly imposes his own needs and opinions onto the child without leaving any room for the child's own preferences to unfold, which is often done in a seemingly loving manner. *I am doing this because I love you* becomes the modus operandi, which leaves the child no choice but to comply with what is expected of him, and his own sense of self remains undeveloped. The child is condemned to passivity and learns to leave it up to others to make decisions.

An insecure parent who suffers from a lot of anxiety himself will sometimes try to gloss over his own sense of instability by constantly checking in with the child. Feeling empty and chronically unsure of how to deal with a newborn, an overly anxious parent will nervously watch every movement of the infant, for fear he or she may do something wrong. The parent's own sense of insecurity becomes a part of the child's emotional organization, manifesting in the child a constant watchfulness of others, hoping that they will provide some clues of what would be the right thing to do, while failing to develop core values and self-esteem with the help of a stronger, more stable caregiver.

Other parents, who haven't been sufficiently nurtured by their own mothers and fathers, try to use their child as a means to finally get the attention and care they missed out on in their own upbringing. Some of these children become their mother's or father's best friends and confidantes, and they have to carry the needs of the parents, as opposed to the other way around. In extreme cases, it might happen, for example, that an eight-year-old has to make important decisions for the overwhelmed mother, a dynamic that is defined as child abuse in many states in the U.S. The child is being robbed of a self that hasn't had the chance to develop enough to nurture a fragile parent; the child remains overburdened and weakened in her own sense of self. All these examples of faulty parenting are representations of what is called *misattunement*: a profound lack of understanding of what the child really needs, as opposed to what the parents think the child needs.

Kohut divided these narcissistic personalities into several categories, the most important of which are the under-stimulated, the over-stimulated, and the overburdened selves. Most people who are fragile and vulnerable in their core belong to one of these. Children who grow up in an under-stimulating environment were put on the back burner of family life and parental attention. They remained in the background when the goodies were handed out, held still when an injury had to be treated, spoke up only when asked, and even then said only the most necessary things. Because of this restraint, they often experience themselves as boring or even dead, and some start to seek stimulation by going to extremes later in life. They look for a physical thrill, like skydiving or bungee jumping. Some experience devastating arguments and fights as stimulating when it is the only source of vitality in their lives. More self-destructive personalities will resort to drugs, gambling, promiscuity or alcohol to provide them with a stimulating emotional experience. This kind of acting out is also used as distraction from unwanted feelings like anxiety or depression. Under-stimulated children might spend long parts of their days alone without any energizing influence and thus learn to always keep their life force on a low flame. There is no one there with whom to share their experiences or to infuse some extra energy into them. Their creative and intellectual capabilities might never unfold fully because no one shows interest, or worse, the family discourages the child from any kind of self expression. They are never taught how to engage others and remain passive and withdrawn.

On the contrary, the over-stimulated self feels overwhelmed and intruded upon by the parents in ways that don't promote development. The mother may have been unable to soothe the child when he was crying and instead continuously tried to distract him from the pain. Parking a child in front of the TV when she is distressed will teach her that the only means to deal with pain is to not deal with it. This way the child has no chance to accept disappointment as a normal part of life. Instead she comes to believe that pain has to be avoided at all costs, at worst with destructive means like using drugs or overeating.

Over-stimulated children tend to feel crowded because they are overly or inappropriately mirrored, that is, their parents try to convey to their children what they think is going on with them, but never truly understand. This may lead later to confusion as to what the child wants from life. These children might have had a dominating, powerful or famous parent whose glamour overshadowed the child's need to shine. There was no calming presence that would have enabled the child to develop self-soothing mechanisms. One or both parents may have been very anxious or overbearing personalities who constantly worried about the child without giving her room to experiment and explore. Perhaps the parents tried to push sex education on their little boy too early or constantly pried into his relationship with the other parent. The child may have been overwhelmed with too much education or the unattainable demand to become a sports star by his ambitious parents, and had no other choice but to withdraw and avoid even more stimuli—regardless of whether he lived up to their expectations or not.

Over-stimulated selves may come to feel that everything they try to accomplish is doomed to fail, that their own lack of discipline or determination will undermine any accomplishment, and that they were robbed of a certain vigor and strength they crave and admire in others. They search for calm and peace and discover that they have no inner resources of their own, once they are left to their own devices. The danger later in life is that these personalities become stuck in an environment that lacks any stimulation at all, and they experience their lives as empty and boring. They see their own or their parents' grandiose visions of their future as a burden; they become anxious and flooded with emotion because they feel that they have already failed and are afraid of more failures. As adults, these children often have great difficulty pursuing their goals for fear of being overwhelmed again.

In popular culture, the *South Park* character Tweek is an example. Tweek, whose parents run a coffee shop, is literally permanently over-stimulated because the daily diet of this eight-year-old consists of massive amounts of coffee. "Have a cup," the father will say when Tweek, who is always shaking, is unnerved by some dispute among the children. All you hear from him is his hysterical trademark shriek and you see him running off. In one episode he wakes up in the middle of the night to some kind of authority banging on his bedroom door, warning him that a child abuser is out to get him. When, as ordered, he slowly stumbles to the door and opens it to get away, it is the father who holds a gun to his head, yelling "Bang. You are dead. Haven't we told you to never open the door to anyone but your mother and me?" Psychoanalytically speaking, Tweek is driven out of his mind by too much of everything, most of all his parents' craziness and the absence of a soothing person whom he trusts and with whom he can rest.

Overburdened personalities feel unsupported and can't shake the feeling that they are responsible for everything and that they can't be bothered with anything anymore. They turn out to be hypersensitive to any kind of stimulus. They might constantly complain about the weather, about having to do chores, about having to work too much, about having to adjust their schedules to other peoples' needs. They are hypersensitive and tend to take any casual remark as an insult and often become preoccupied with their health and their bodies or turn into hypochondriacs. They never had the chance to enjoy the calmness of a mature caretaker and were instead always pointed to when it came to chores no one else wanted to do.

They are taken over often by anxiety and the ongoing fear of not being up to the task. This manifests itself particularly in relationships: When a child was always responsible for attending to the parents' needs he may come to believe that this is what he has to do for his girlfriend or spouse as well. But because he unconsciously feels overburdened and doesn't know how to ask for his own needs to be met, he engages only in shallow relationships and shies away from any kind of commitment, out of fear of being taken advantage of all over again. He may go on, constantly looking for "someone better" who will finally understand his needs. If at the same time he is afraid of being alone, he may end up cheating on his partner in the hope of finally having found a new love who will know what he needs. But without knowing for himself what his needs are, he is doomed to fail.

When ongoing, all these narcissistic injuries result in a weakened and fragile self that is easily swayed and vulnerable to more hurt. These three types of narcissism are not always so clear cut. Sometimes one person can turn out to be under-stimulated and yet overburdened by expectations at the same time. The gentle narcissists is often the good girl or good boy of the family, always stepping back when someone else demands attention, trained to cater to the needs of the parents or siblings. Because nobody ever seemed to wonder or really understand what this fragile little person wanted, and because she mostly paid attention to what other people needed, she is having trouble later in life knowing what she wants. She doesn't know whether to pursue this or that career path, whether to give in to the courtship of this man or another, live in this town or the next. The basic problem with all these chronic child-rearing failures is that one way or another they communicate to the child: *Something is wrong with you. You don't live up to my expectations. I don't like the way you are. You really should be different.* The psychologist Stephen Johnson put it this way: "When what you are is too much or too little, too sexual, or not sexual enough, too stimulating or not stimulating enough, too precocious or too slow, too independent or not independent enough, you cannot freely realize yourself. *That* is the narcissistic injury."

On the flip side, as a parent or psychotherapist, one has to wonder just how many mistakes we are making all day long trying to raise children — and treat patients, for that matter. We all make many mistakes. But it's not about the occasional failure to provide the best care possible. To some extent it's even necessary that children learn how imperfectly the world treats them, because this is what awaits them as adults, and they need to learn how to cope with it. It's all about the right balance. What's important is that we provide them with an overall stable environment and with a set of morals and values that we teach them by being role models, not by feeding them a constant diet of what's right and wrong or by ignoring what they have to bring to the table. And, even more crucially, we have to demonstrate that a screw-up can always be repaired. Even if you do forget your son's soccer tournament, you can make up for it by allowing him to complain and by showing up the next time.

Many people feel uncomfortable blaming their parents or caretakers for what they believe are their own inadequacies. So instead they blame themselves, complaining that they should have gotten over any childhood traumas. It is hard for them to see anybody else's contribution to their misery, and they put it solely upon themselves to right what's been wronged. But the truth is, assigning blame is an essential part of every social system, including the family, as a tool to achieve justice. When a child kicks the dog to act out his own anger, he will get punished for it. When the father kicks the dog, he most likely will get away with it, because most children — especially when they are fragile and forced to please the parents — won't point their finger at the almighty adult, even less so when the father kicks the child himself. The sense that injustice took place may linger for many years and won't disappear until it is rectified or acknowledged as such. And while there are many forms in which blame can be expressed, the sheer act of assigning blame becomes an important part of the functioning of relationships because it enables the process of repair. As the sociologist Charles Tilly has argued: "Blame occurs in public debate, in courts, and in everyday life. Although the word 'justice' alone often calls up a warm glow, justice commonly consists first of fixing blame, then of imposing penalties for blame. More so than the giving of credit, assigning blame can easily become a persistent, destructive habit. Many a friendship, partnership, and marriage break up over the assignment of blame. But when carried out successfully through retaliation, incapacitation, deterrence, rehabilitation or restoration, blaming brings struggles to an end."

4. Hallmark Characteristics of the Gentle Self

Avoidance

Avoiding difficult situations like conflict in a relationship is a typical characteristic of the gentle self. We have learned to build up our defenses and prefer to avoid people and situations that make us feel uncomfortable. Who wants to confront a friend who has overstepped our boundaries? Who wouldn´t prefer to end a relationship that has gone sour by email rather than by talking to the other person? Sometimes avoidance is exactly what we have to do to survive in a difficult environment, but other times we go overboard in trying to protect ourselves. This is when we shut out others and shut ourselves down and don't want to look at who we actually are. Underneath all the defenses and distractions we are actually vulnerable creatures.

Withdrawal and avoidance are a part of our society. Who doesn't have a friend who reacts to our emails and phone calls only belatedly or not at all? Who hasn't dealt with difficult interpersonal situations at home or work by *not* dealing with them? Some prefer to hold a grudge against someone for a decade rather than spell out the hurtful business with that person. Not everyone who acts like this is necessarily withdrawn. And verbalizing frustration is not always the solution for an already damaged relationship, especially when it is brought up in an angry tone. But we have to consider that there is a chance the avoider is not calling back not because he is uncaring or mean, but because he feels overwhelmed by the demands he thinks are placed on him and — consciously or unconsciously — might even feel inadequate or unworthy of your friendship.

Many people avoid others out of fear of rejection. I once had a colleague who barricaded himself behind his desk, claiming to do urgent work, when the office party was about to start. He stood around awkwardly, clinging to one person he felt somewhat comfortable with, and then left without saying good-bye, thinking or hoping that no one would notice. At times he became cynical about the purpose of such a gathering, blaming the organizers for being self-involved, while at the same time he craved nothing more than to be acknowledged by his peers in the same fashion. What he was unaware of was that his friends and colleagues were baffled by his standoffish behavior, wondering what in the world may have caused the sudden retreat, and felt hurt and angry — for being ignored, neglected, or stood up.

What we tormented gentle introverts don't realize, of course, is that we do have something to offer. We often have a soothing nature that makes our more wound-up contemporaries feel under less pressure. We often wrongfully feel as if we have nothing to say and tend to ask a lot of questions, which in turn makes the other person feel welcome and interesting. Many of us end up in the arts or a creative profession or have at least a keen interest in one of those fields; we do have our own perspective to contribute that is different and often more thought-out than others' quick comments.

Sometimes those seemingly more outgoing colleagues are even envious of the achievements of their withdrawn coworkers.

Some of us not only physically retreat from the world but also withdraw by being absentminded, by daydreaming and even by sleeping. Some sleep through weekends or long into the day and become active at night because this way they simply aren't present when others knock on their doors, wanting time or things they are not ready to give. It is difficult for many of us to say straightforwardly that we are not available, and we prefer to invent excuses and mishaps to avoid people we don't feel at ease with or dreaded confrontations we fear will make us the target of aggression we are not equipped to handle.

Some people tune out by tuning in to music, most effectively with the help of an iPod, while riding a crowded train or when trying to get away from someone. One of my clients prefers to exercise by swimming laps in a pool at six in the morning when no one is there. She describes how much she loves the feeling of being completely with herself, a temporary illusion that is enhanced by dipping her head under during the monotonous strokes, listening to the sound of her breath exhaling into the water, being one with the rhythm of her movements. It can be a perfect form of solitude, of fully occupying the body—and also a way of being totally in your head.

Being bogged down by parents, bosses, partners, children or a whole group—and mostly by one´s own expectations—is where depression often comes from. These can include feeling obligated to maintain the family peace or holding to work morale although it goes against your own needs; feeling too fragile and dependent to stand up for yourself; being mired in conflict between what others expect and what you need for yourself; not feeling you have the right or the strength to put your foot down; being afraid to hurt someone else more than yourself; putting the other first. This is what depression often is: suppressing one´s own point of view for the benefit of the other, not being able or not wanting to be "selfish."

Our bodies speak of our depression. Physical signs of sadness and hopelessness are often hunched or raised shoulders, as if we have to duck away from abuse or retreat inwards. Shoulder tension often leads to headaches and chronic neck or back pain. Many have an overall stiff body or a frozen appearance, others a tight or constricted diaphragm that prevents them from breathing fully, or a rigidly held pelvis which can indicate sexual inhibitions. Many people, especially women, have a high-pitched, childlike voice, a physical sign of their involuntary smallness.

Feelings of worthlessness and self-effacing or downright self-destructive behavior are common occurrences. Because many of us gentle narcissists feel useless and unwanted, we often remain shy and passive towards others. We have a hard time making demands when another person doesn't seem to agree, or, even more so, we are unable show anger at other people's inconsiderateness. We become "sneaky" and find indirect ways to get what we want or become passive-aggressive. It is important to understand that this behavior is not caused by malicious intent, but that many gentle selves have no other choice but to evade difficult situations in order to protect their weakened sense of self, either from being taken over or from further injury. Nurturing self-esteem and supporting their decisions is crucial for us to become more proactive in life.

One of my clients suffered from severe depression for years. Charlotte´s parents were genuinely caring but were unable to provide her with the strong role model and the structure she needed. Her father was self-absorbed, and his romanticized pleas for love and openness in relationships were never sufficiently focused on his daughter´s needs and proved ultimately intrusive and overbearing. The mother, a self-effacing and submissive personality, communicated to her daughter that directing attention to herself was unacceptable, and she failed to be an empowering role model. Charlotte had no sense of agency, feeling powerless and unmotivated and unable to identify or pursue any meaningful professional goals. She felt chronically depressed for many years of her life. Her undeveloped sense of self was in need of a role model of strength and determination whom she could admire and live up to.

Over time, she became aware that she needed to separate from her chaotic father. As an adult, she couldn't allow him to be an important part of her life anymore, because he would inevitably only complain about how she didn't pay him enough attention, while all along he had never really listened to her. She limited her contact with him drastically and was therefore able to diminish much of the self-loathing his irrational blame triggered in her. Little by little, she developed the confidence to pursue her own goals, independent of what her father would think of them, and became a successful healthcare professional.

Another client I had felt trapped between the wishes of her husband and her lover. Her husband wanted her to stay in the marriage while the lover wanted her to split up. When she did some soul searching, she understood that she needed more time to clarify for herself what it would mean to her if she would stay or go. The plain exploration of her needs, however, did not bring about any relief. The insight that she always tried to accommodate the needs of the men in her life—as she always used to accommodate her father's wishes—made her angry. This anger enabled her to focus on herself rather than on what others needed and liberated her from her depressive mood.

Many people who are depressed and feel that they have no means to impact their relationships seek distraction or comfort in worldly remedies like food or alcohol. Overeating is perhaps the most accepted and currently the most prevalent way of seeking comfort, when one's energy reservoir is depleted and there is no one there to ease the pain. Substances like sugar or salt have been proven to have a comforting or satisfying effect and are frequently used to compensate for emotional pain. When you find yourself falling into a depressed mood and start overeating or drinking, ask yourself what you would really need in order to feel better. Very often it goes back to having (or rather not having) one's needs for attention and support met. Do you need the attention of a friend to cope with your sadness? Do you feel left out by a group or overwhelmed by someone's expectations? It's essential to be aware of those needs and how to go about satisfying them. Many people think that drawing attention to them is "selfish" or inappropriate. They have been told or made to believe in the past that they need to hold their heads down, stop bragging and keep any form of desire for attention to themselves. But getting the right kind of attention you need is crucial to your emotional well being. Don't be afraid to ask for it.

General Anxiety and Social Anxiety

Anxiety or stress is a minor form of fragmentation, i.e., the fear of falling apart, not being able to hold it together any more. We are afraid that we can't live up to the expectations of our bosses, our partners and ourselves. Sometimes anxiety is covered up or compensated for by all kinds of compulsions: nail biting, scab picking or pimple popping are preferred compulsive expressions of general anxiety. Others go further, scrubbing their hands, bodies or apartments incessantly. Even hoarding can be seen as an outlet for anxiety and the fear of letting go. Some act out by taking drugs or spending too much money while shopping, or drinking or eating too much. We worry constantly about our homes, our jobs, our loved ones. Especially at night we are particularly vulnerable to all kinds of fears. We have trouble sleeping and roll around in bed, convinced that all the worst case scenarios we can come up with in our anxious minds will inevitably come true.

Not that we are alone in this. Studies reveal that up to one-third of all Americans will develop some kind of anxiety disorder during their lives. The United States is perhaps the most anxious industrial nation in the world, and more so than any developing country, which is not surprising when we consider the defense mechanism that always comes with anxiety: control. We want to be able to have control over our circumstances, our relationships and our feelings at all times. We have learned to say "yes, we can" and "there´s nothing I can't accomplish if I just put my mind to it." It´s the American way.

Unfortunately, the mind and body are oblivious to this kind of attempted self-empowerment. Thoughts cannot be controlled easily; we can only become aware of them and try to refocus them. We are unable to prevent our minds from having bad dreams or feeling sad at times. Mind control is a modern myth that is very popular because of its seductiveness. But we simply are unable to erase the thoughts and memories from our brains. We have to deal with them, like it or not. Our bodies, too, can only be controlled up to a certain point. We can push them to their limits with diligent discipline, but we can´t avoid getting older, getting sick and eventually dying. Modern science is trying its best to delay and prevent death. But this is the ultimate test— we have to give up control and just face our fear.

Many gentle narcissists suffer from anxiety, especially from social anxiety. We don't feel comfortable in social situations that consist of more than a handful of people. As soon as a group gets too large to hold the attention of even one participant, we tend to get that creeping feeling of anxiety: the chance of being overheard and overlooked or sometimes simultaneously being overwhelmed grows dramatically, which puts us back into the well-known situation of the original trauma we suffered as children. With this renewed dread of being neglected or not really understood — however benign it may be in a particular social context — grows our sense of being pushed out of the spotlight. We lose the connection to those we wanted to address and our voices falter and trail off. We may feel discouraged by the belief that nothing we have to say is unique or funny or intelligent enough, and we fall silent as if we weren't there anymore. The feeling of being the outsider of the group is inevitable.

A curious expression of social anxiety seems to be an intense dislike of talking on the phone. Gentle narcissists often prefer either email, text messaging or meeting face to face rather than picking up the phone. They may be afraid of not really being paid attention to, that the interpersonal connection might get too tenuous, or of being held on the phone while their conversation partner is preoccupied with other things. The physical expression of being heard and seen, the attentive body language, the eye contact are missing, which creates a vague fear of not really being paid attention to.

One of my clients, George, frequently struggled with his feelings of emptiness and insecurity when he was around his wife's extended family. He would come along for a holiday gathering, and although everyone was welcoming and friendly, he felt nearly paralyzed when it came to actively connecting with someone. He found himself sitting at the dinner table, occasionally commenting on what was being talked about, but unable to address anybody personally or directly. "It's like I can't think of a single thing to say," he observed, and he frequently resorted to alcohol to soothe his anxiety.

George felt excluded by all the children in the family, who were receiving the attention he craved for himself, and he could never muster the courage to engage with them himself. He felt alone in the group because he felt that the group was closing in on him and taking over and pushing aside whatever he had to contribute. One day five of the family members, including himself, went on a trip into the wilderness together, an environment of peace and quiet that usually enabled him to engage. But he still found himself dumbfounded by his social paralysis. A surprising thing happened when one of them had to leave and the four remaining people went on with their trip. "All off a sudden I felt visible, and I became alive," he told me. "My anxiety could handle three other people, but it drew the line at four."

What often happens in a situation that triggers social anxiety is that we lost, or never really had, the support and validation of someone who really appreciated or listened to us, of another social being who made us feel like we had something meaningful to contribute to whatever was going on. As soon as those eyes turn away by some distraction, we lose the ground we've just been standing on. The longer we go without any self-sustaining attention from another person, the deeper we tend to fall into a hole of self-doubt and fear, and the harder it gets to dig ourselves out of it. We feel as though our inner structure is weakening and crumbling, and in order to prevent complete collapse, we need to get away from the overwhelming situation and regain a sense of ourselves in a safe place, where we are in control and no one else can take over.

The flip side of the fear of not being heard or seen is to be afraid of being taken over by someone, which threatens to obliterate the shy person's personality. In order to avoid getting too close to someone, withdrawn individuals don't just appear physically and emotionally aloof, they simply want to hide from people—if not physically then emotionally. They hide their feelings or put on a tough poker face, they hide their vulnerabilities to avoid getting hurt, and sometimes they hide their whole physical self in order to evade overwhelming situations.

At the same time, we crave nothing more than for someone to come to our rescue and reach out to us and include us. Kohut writes: "Contact shunning personalities may well be the most frequent of the narcissistic character types, not because they are disinterested in others, but, on the contrary, just because of their need for them is so intense. The intensity of their need not only leads to great sensitivity to rejection—but also, on a deeper, unconscious level, to the apprehension that the remnants of their nuclear self will be swallowed up and destroyed by the yearned-for, all-encompassing union."

More severe forms of withdrawal, social isolation, and the inability to form lasting relationships suggest that the child felt rejected or intruded upon not just by one but by both parents and potentially by other family members early on. Psychoanalytic theory indicates that in this character formation a symbiotic relationship between the infant and the mother (or caregiver) never took place—whether because the mother was preoccupied, or overwhelmed by having to deal with a helpless being who depended solely on her—the reasons for this are many. She may simply have not been there, because she was sick or had to work around the clock, or was incapable of caring for someone else. She may have been an alcoholic who had no capacity to take care of anyone, including herself.

She may have been someone who withdrew from everybody, including her own children. She may have been depressed or anxiety-ridden herself or otherwise mentally ill, with or without anyone ever diagnosing it. She may have had what felt like an overwhelming need for someone to fill the void in her own emotional organization, for someone who would love her unconditionally, and could not give real love to her child. Whatever the deficit was that the child had to cope with, to the child it ultimately felt like rejection and neglect—not really being heard; not being paid attention to; not being comforted when afraid; not having physical needs met; or actively being put down, ridiculed, cursed, beaten, or completely forgotten. The plain absence of genuine love and care equals abandonment, and the act of rejection is experienced as traumatic.

The earlier such an emotional or physical absence of the caregiver occurs—and when there is no one else who can fill the void—the more likely it is that the child will believe that she is undeserving of a person's attention. "The child comes to feel that she is not really loved for herself as a person by her mother, and that her own love for her mother is not really valued by her," argues British psychoanalyst Ronald Fairbairn. With no place to put her own love and needs, she learns to keep them to herself, becoming convinced that her needs really are too much to take, and that she can't expect anyone to give her what she desires. She is certain that if she were to make her needs heard, she would be misunderstood, ignored, rejected or altogether left behind. So she learns to stay at a distance, not wanting anything, not needing anything, not asking for too much, always ready to preemptively cut herself off from what she wants, so that no one else can do this to her.

Low Self-esteem

Low self esteem is common among gentle selves and with it come all forms of self-defeat, self-effacement, self-deprecation, and self-loathing. Holding the self in such low regard is typical of this personality type. Because of their low opinion of themselves, gentle narcissists often believe — sometimes unconsciously — that their presence is genuinely unwanted: that they waste other people's time, that they aren't likable, that something is wrong with them, that they want too much, that they have to apologize constantly for their behavior, their needs, the fact that they are there.

We have a deep-rooted sense of having some kind of deficit that needs to be covered up in order to protect ourselves, a belief that we are somehow not enough the way we are. So we withdraw. But our withdrawn demeanor pushes away people who care for us, which forces us further onto the path of self-isolation. Once we begin to see that this is what we are doing, we can begin to stop running away from others and see how they do enjoy being with us, how much they value our friendship and that we are lovable and worth the effort.

For many years, psychotherapists and psycho-analytic theory have been calling all forms of self-defeat "masochism," a term that is still associated with the practice of seeking pain or humiliation in sexual encounters as a means to find erotic pleasure or to reach orgasm. And there certainly are people who manipulate others at their own expense for the sake of achieving some twisted sense of satisfaction or revenge. For example, some religious fundamentalists torture themselves in many different ways, not just physically but also emotionally, in the clandestine belief in their own superiority over non-believers. But there is no pleasure in the gentle narcissist's need to put the self second. There is only despair and a deep-seated fear of losing people who are vital to them, because this loss would mean unbearable pain and the inevitable falling apart. Associating this suffering with a masochistic joy in pain completely misses the point.

I used to work with a young woman named Jessica whose mother was an alcoholic and whose father was a deeply withdrawn and cold personality. As a child, she spent large portions of the day by herself when her parents went to work, and she received attention from them only by being screamed at or reprimanded. She was neglected and isolated throughout most of her childhood and learned early that her presence wasn't welcome in her parents' house. She became a deeply withdrawn young woman who formed only superficial relationships that were easily discarded. Even though she grew up around the family, she unconsciously felt that she had been rejected and abandoned by the most important people in her life and that this was her fault because she must have been a deeply unlovable child.

Jessica´s behavioral patterns were dominated by what some psychoanalysts call an "organizing principle": a powerful belief about ourselves, which we are usually unaware of, that stems from how we were treated early in our childhood and that organizes our relationships and continues throughout our lives. It constantly lingers in the background when we try to form new relationships and when we abandon old ones, and it becomes a silent whisper in just about everything we do.

Jessica was convinced that she wasn't lovable, that she was a nuisance to everyone, that she didn't deserve a loving relationship with a partner and had to take what she could get. She tended to team up with cold personalities like her father, because for her, this was normalcy. She was used to being turned down and yelled at, and so she came to expect this treatment from her boyfriends. At some point, these relationships usually erupted in violence, either verbally or physically. Strangely, to her these shouting matches had a ring of aliveness to them because of the under-stimulating environment she grew up in and as an adult chose to live in. All she got to see all day long as a child was the stifling deadness of her parents' overstuffed house. Any sense of excitement or joy, even just a little simple human contact, was missing. The only feeling came in the form of both her mother's and her father's verbal attacks on her and each other. Thus fighting became a rare yet destructive source of excitement for Jessica.

Because she never experienced the warmth and care of parental love, she felt generally distrustful and undeserving of the love other people tried to offer her. Romance was difficult for her to take, because she was never sure whether to trust the sweet words that she heard, and sometimes she felt simply ridiculed by them because they sounded so far out. Each of her blossoming new relationships inevitably ended in disaster, sometimes brought on by her partner's unavailability and sometimes by her own deep-seated fear of rejection and feelings of inadequacy.

People who were equally deprived of love and the most basic care in childhood fare best by seeking psychotherapy because they need a lot of nurturing and understanding. But less dramatic and destructive forms of this dynamic occur in many relationships. We crave love and intimacy but have trouble getting close to someone because we see rejection in the most random act or remark, and then we disengage. How many times does a second date not even happen because both parties involved believe that they came across as "lame" or "ugly" or "uninteresting"? Most likely none of the above was true. Nobody dared to find out, for fear that the inevitable rejection would be too hurtful. How often have we avoided a social get-together out of a belief that no one there would find us interesting or would enjoy having us there? How many friendships never reach a certain intimacy because we are convinced that calling more often would come across as annoying or needy? How often do we demand that the other person make more of an effort?

Paradoxically, the belief that we are not good enough may not only arise from rejection but also from generally well-meaning yet inappropriate expectations. Briana was a young woman who could barely stand herself: She was extremely driven and always excelled in everything she attempted, whether it was her career as an administrative assistant, her quest in finding the perfect mate, her hobby as a dog walker or scrubbing her house as close to germfree as humanly possible. However, none of her successes gave her any joy. She felt inadequate if she made the slightest mistake at her job, dumped any guy who wasn´t the perfect gentleman, felt responsible when her dog wouldn´t do what she wanted him to, and frequently turned on her body for any pound she gained and every pimple that made an appearance. She was afraid of contracting any kind of disease and kept herself and her house as clean as she could.

Briana was a single child and the apple of her mother´s eye. As a kid she would be dressed up and paraded in front of the neighbors even though she felt embarrassed by her mother making a fuss over her. Her mother assured her that she was the most important person in her life and her best friend. She bought all the clothes and books and vacations her daughter could ever desire. She constantly tried to reassure Briana of her beauty and intelligence, even when she came home on a bad-hair-day or with a failed exam. Briana felt as if she was never really heard when she tried to articulate her needs and was not taken seriously when she had self-doubts, which were habitually brushed off as irrational. When Briana tried to stand up for herself, and wore pants instead of skirts and listened to punk instead of country music, her mother would burst into tears and wonder aloud what she had done wrong.

Briana came to believe deeply that something was wrong with her, that she wasn't good enough just as she was, but that she had to prove herself over and over again. Just as her own quirks and idiosyncrasies weren't acceptable to the mother, she couldn't fall for anyone who was less than perfect, because she needed to be with someone she could admire for something she was incapable of doing herself. Because her standards for herself and others were too high for any ordinary human to live up to, she felt chronically like a failure and pushed away other imperfect people, not knowing who she was or was supposed to be. The only thing Briana knew was that she wasn't good enough to herself or to her mother, who verbally told her how perfect she was but couldn't tolerate that her daughter was really different from how she wanted her to be.

These examples of Jessica and Briana show how much our behavior is influenced by beliefs about ourselves. Jessica chose unavailable love interests out of a deep conviction that she wasn't wanted and didn't deserve better, and she rejected the notion of romantic love because she felt she couldn't give what was asked of her. Briana was certain that she wasn't good enough the way she was but dealt with it by constantly having to prove that she could do better than anyone else.

Many gentle narcissists don´t quite know what they want, much less how to get it. For them, the easiest solution in any situation of conflict is to go along with what is demanded of them. They want to please their parents, their in-laws, their bosses and colleagues by agreeing with their stances, by not making any trouble and hoping to avoid conflict and arguments down the road. The problem is that sooner or later they get the creeping feeling that things never go their way, that it´s always the others whose opinions seem more valuable and who speak up louder than they do. They might be upset that they always get the short end of the stick and yet feel incapable of making themselves heard. Or they are too afraid of the repercussions of disagreeing and give in without ever putting up a fight. Or they may simply not quite know how to feel about a particular decision and just nod along with everybody else.

Because the environment they grew up in forces them to behave according to the expectations of our caretakers, many gentle narcissists develop what British psychoanalyst Donald Winnicott called a "false self." They believe that adjusting to others is the only thing they have to offer and comply with what they think is expected of us. They often don´t dare to voice spontaneously their true feelings out of fear of being rejected or abandoned or put down, and wait for others to react first so they can join in.
Francis, a young woman I worked with for many years, fit the pattern perfectly. She grew up with a depressed father who had little interest in his

children, a weak and compliant mother, and a tyrannical uncle who ran the family business and whom Francis´ parents depended upon. She learned early that her needs were not important within the family structure, and she suppressed every desire for attention, encouragement and emotional support. Francis remembered what can be called a "model scene," that is, an emotionally incisive moment that encapsulates a recurring pattern. It happened when she was three or four years old: She was waiting for her father to come home from work and stood anxiously in the doorway to greet him. When he arrived, he barely noticed her and immediately went downstairs to the basement where he withdrew to refurbish furniture, a hobby that seemed to be the only source of satisfaction for him but which didn´t include his children or allow for any kind of family social life.

Francis came to feel that her father had no joy or interest in his daughter´s development and felt like a nuisance. Her mother, who struggled with her own inability to make her interests known in the face of an indifferent spouse and the domineering uncle, proved to be a poor role model who communicated to Francis that it was pointless to even try to speak up for herself. The uncle, who had no patience with Francis and burst out in anger about every little mishap, intimidated her and forced her to display the only kind of behavior he seemed to respond to, namely pleasing him by not being "difficult." For Francis, this meant not asking for anything, working hard for the family business without being rewarded or praised for it and generally staying out of his way.

Francis left her hometown right after finishing high school. Unconsciously, she was looking for a supportive environment where she would receive more attention and acceptance. Although she was able to find friends and completed her education, in romantic relationships she always followed the lead of her often overbearing and controlling partners. Inevitably, these relationships were doomed to fail, which they did after Francis withdrew from them without ever spelling out what was going wrong.

A similar dynamic unfolded with her friends and colleagues. She started to notice how things went smoothly as long as she agreed with everybody and no conflicts arose. But as soon as disagreements occurred she found herself compromising the situation. "If it´s not going to work out, I´ll find another job or move to another town" was a habitual thought when a difficult dynamic at work required an open discussion. The same thing started to happen with friends. "If she continues to blame me for not being in touch, we just won´t be friends anymore," she thought frequently.

It didn´t cross her mind that changing her workplace for the sake of avoiding conflict jeopardized the connections she had made. Furthermore, she would have to adjust to yet another company and another set of colleagues. The ongoing loss of friends made Francis feel depleted and lonely, and over the years it became harder and harder to find a whole new set of social contacts and to get used to another city with its own distinctive geography and culture. Eventually, she met someone who encouraged her to articulate her thoughts honestly, who did not turn against her when her feelings proved to be complex and difficult to bear for her; this enabled her to negotiate her position and feel more engaged in the relationship. Over time she was able to shake off the almost compulsive need to be pleasant and accommodating to everyone, which was her variation of Winnicott´s false self. She learned that there were people who could tolerate it when she stepped out of her role as a "good girl" and didn't punish her for it, which made her feel accepted and increased her desire to be genuinely supportive of her partner´s strivings, instead of just paying lip service to him.

The need to please can arise from overly strict parents as well as from overly praiseful ones. "An evaluative atmosphere of perpetual praise and applause is equally damaging to the development of realistic self-esteem," writes psychoanalyst Nancy McWilliams. "The child is always aware of being judged, even if the verdict is positive. He or she knows on some level that there is a false quality to the attitude of constant admiration, and despite the conscious sense of entitlement that may issue from such a background, it creates the nagging worry that one is a bit of a fraud, undeserving of this adulation that seems tangential to who one really is."

Perfectionism

The fantasy and the pursuit of perfection are a part of Western culture, especially in the United States, because it is seen as a virtue, as a desirable goal in life. We are bombarded with images of beautiful bodies, perfect teeth, perfect skin. Plastic surgeons and aestheticians are in high demand. Others substitute professional or athletic goals for the perfect appearance. Being number one is the highest honor and we construct our lives around it. We want to climb the ladder of corporate and academic success and be seen and acknowledged for our skill, and we can´t stop wanting to be even better. Perfectionism doesn´t stop at relationships. We want to have the most beautiful wedding, the ideal partner, perfect children and grandchildren. We are perfectionists in our jobs, not wanting to give up control for fear someone else will mess it up. We spend our lives constantly trying to improve our work, our hobbies and ourselves.

The dream of perfection is a hallmark characteristic of the narcissistic personality. We are unhappy with our noses, our friends, our spouses, our job performance. If we can´t have it ourselves, we want to be seen and associated with someone else who is perfect — someone with a perfect body, the best reputation, the largest bank account. Ideas of perfection don´t just serve to bolster expressions of grandeur. In the case of the gentle self, they usually serve as fantasies to cover up or substitute for anxiety or depression about the less pleasurable aspects of life, or what is felt to be an inherently deficient personality. If I can hold on to the idea that I am striving to be the best football player in town, I can avoid my feelings of inferiority about having a small penis. If only I had a girlfriend with a perfect body so I don´t have to feel so bad about being unable to hold a job. If I create the perfect presentation at my job, people will appreciate me despite my social awkwardness. These fantasies are (often unconsciously) used to deflect from wounds that have occurred both in childhood and later in life. For example, a destructive relationship with a parent is compensated for by the goal of becoming the best lawyer in town; the hope really is that the father will finally approve of his son. Another example is when the emotional consequences of a stifling marriage are suppressed by putting maximum effort into raising the perfect children.

Many adults see their children as a means through which they will finally get what they have missed out on. They want their son to become a tennis pro and bask in his success because they couldn´t pursue their own goals. They don´t want to deal with the fact that their children are genuinely fallible — that they may not be the best in their class, that they may be too weak to stand up to a bully, that they could get sick and grow fearful. These parents don´t want to deal with their children´s failures and imperfections, just as they don´t like them in their own personalities.

The trouble with perfectionism is that it not only prevents us from feeling good about our work and ourselves, it can also lead to an inability to make decisions or finish projects. When only the best is good enough, chances are that the pressure to become the best is too much to even get close to that goal. I worked with a young man, Thomas, who for many years was unable to ever be happy with anything he did because of his own unrealistically high standards for himself. He would procrastinate for a long time before he tackled a job that needed to be done and expected it to turn out flawless. He alienated his teammates whose input he did not accept, and he was unable to give up control of any small detail out of fear the others wouldn't live up to his standards. Nothing he ever did was good enough and it took him an excessive amount of time to finish any project. He ended up losing job after job because of these patterns.

Thomas had grown up with a withholding father who never showed any positive emotion towards him and was impatient with everything he did. When he was learning to ride a bike, his father expected him to master it on the first day and made fun of his clumsy efforts. Thomas came to feel that whatever he did was never going to be good enough and began to strive for perfection so nobody would ever be critical of him again. Thomas' mother was equally perfectionist and needed everything in the house to function without any problem. She became angry when Thomas soiled his clothes at a football game and didn't tolerate any mess at the dinner table, even when it was a harmless mishap. He learned early on that the only way to escape criticism was to deliver a flawless piece of work, which ultimately was still not appreciated by his parents. Thomas could never feel proud of his achievements even if it felt like he did the best anyone could possibly do.

Idealization

Idealization is a normal part of life. As children, we idealize our parents, take on their likes and dislikes, their values and behaviors. Early in life, we look at our parents as idealized and omnipotent, almost God-like figures who seem to be able to make things happen just by snapping their fingers. The child longs to be accepted by and emotionally united with this strong, perfect, powerful creature who should be an indispensable source of inspiration and strength. But if a parent proves to be a rather self-effacing role model who cannot allow herself to shine, it will be difficult for her to accept the child's admiration. If on the other hand she can demonstrate a healthy self-esteem that integrates realistic expectations of what is achievable and what is not, she becomes a positive role model to her children in this way.

Of course, reality has a way of showing us how much we can actually achieve in life, but even a failure is easier to tolerate when we can fall back on a stable sense of self that was created by the calm and soothing reactions our parents provided when we were in distress as babies. The same happens with our idealization of the parents, according to Kohut: "However great our disappointment as we discover the weaknesses and limitations of the idealized figures of our early life, their self-confidence as they carried us when we were babies — via their calm voices or via closeness with their relaxed bodies as they held us — will be retained by us as the nucleus of the strength of our leading ideals and of the calmness we experience as we live our lives under the guidance of our inner goals."

The desire to be inspired by others continues – in an increasingly mature way - throughout life. As students, we look up to a particularly under-standing teacher or coach who works to bring out the best in us and gives us confidence just by believing in us. As adults, we long to find a mate who possesses skills we can admire and learn from, and even in old age we look to doctors or our own children for guidance and support.

But there is a flip side to an exaggerated idealization, and that is contempt. When the people we banked on disappoint us, when they let us down and turn out to be much more human and fallible than we need them to be, we quickly turn away. The friend who was always nurturing and supportive but who became depleted by her own need to please and disappeared from the surface of the planet triggers anger and helplessness. The father who was always a reliable provider but got entangled in a business failure suddenly falls from grace when he can´t ensure his children´s financial stability any more. The spouse who was always a model of health but falls sick with cancer becomes a burden, and we want out.

These dynamics are reinforced by cultural factors. America is an inherently narcissistic society. In no other culture is the desire to idealize so prevalent. Nowhere else can actors and politicians rise so high on the scale of public adoration, and fall so low if they disappoint the expectations of the admiring crowds. Barack Obama was elected as the incarnation of a new hope and a new era but was quickly scorned as a disappointment, in part by his most ardent supporters. Artists like Mel Gibson, Brittney Spears or Charlie Sheen were riding high on the enthusiastic waves of their fans, quickly overestimated their own capacities because of all the positive feedback and inevitably crashed and burned in the anger and contempt of their public judges.

By mindlessly looking up to those whom we perceive as wise and all grown up, we underestimate our own potential. We denigrate our own talents and expect some adored superstar to be the perfect human being. What goes up must come down. We need to learn to appreciate what we have to bring to the table and see others as the flawed and fallible beings that they are. We need to learn to take responsibility for our own failures and stop blaming our role models and idols if they don't fulfill our every desire.

Craving Independence

Many gentle narcissists whose emotional needs as a child were rejected or were insufficiently provided for develop a conviction that they need to be able to take care of themselves and be completely independent. It is difficult for us to rely on someone else and to fall back on others out of fear that our needs will again be rejected or ignored. We have a hard time truly trusting people.

In the U.S. the desire for independence is part of the culture. Everyone has their own car, their own house, their own TV and computer in order to be able to use it at all times. We like our neighbors to stay at a safe distance on the other side of the fence. Many people prefer not to ask anybody for a favor or to share a ride. They don´t want to be a bother and they don´t want to be bothered. They rely on themselves, sometimes into bitter loneliness. What tends to go along with the need for independence is a certain unwillingness or inability to relate to other people´s needs. They have so thoroughly internalized that they have to take care of themselves that it is hard for them to understand that others might function differently and may need support.

Feeling responsible for nobody but themselves makes it difficult to consider the point of view of the other. Once they are in an intimate relationship, the routine of doing things their way clashes with the lifestyle of the partner. Often the gentle narcissist, so used to relying only on herself, is unable to hear what the other has to offer and can´t accept that her partner wants to do something for her. She stubbornly sees any input or advice as interference and a threat to her fragile self and fends off any assistance. When her partner then gets frustrated and angry the inevitable clash occurs. The conviction that she doesn´t want to bother anyone else with her needs becomes a point of contention, because the other person feels that he has no impact on her.

Many gentle narcissists avoid corporate jobs and prefer to be self-employed because it is difficult for us to tolerate or counter another person's criticism and because of our need for greater independence. This allows us to have greater control over how to go about our day — and whom we want to deal with. We can keep a greater distance from our bosses, employers and employees. Although some grapple with the lack of structure and self-motivation, many are very driven and successful in their careers and thrive on the freedom and independence one's own business or an independent contractor position provides.

Another dynamic underlying the gentle narcissists' desire for independence is often the conviction that they have nothing to offer. They fear that as soon as someone comes close to them, they will inevitably discover that there is nothing lovable behind their facade, that they have nothing to say and nothing to give and are about to be outed as a fraud. Because the consequence of what feels like an inevitable discovery will again be rejection, it's better not to get involved in the first place. Why set yourself up for disappointment when the letdown is just around the corner? The reason behind this dynamic, which can result in outright fear of commitment, is a deep and often unconscious feeling of a lack of self-worth, a negative self-image that makes it impossible to allow anyone to come close for fear that they might be deemed unworthy and thus be rejected and abandoned all over again.

Jessica, for example, preferred to see her isolation as "independence," as her own choice to stay away from annoying relationships. When she did start to engage with a romantic partner, she immediately felt that unreasonable demands were being made and that she wasn´t able to give anything in return. Even the request of taking care of her partner when he was sick felt like an undue burden that intruded into her daily routine. She ultimately saw even the relationship to her spiritual teacher as too threatening, was afraid of becoming too dependent, and could not allow herself to form any relational ties at all. Her artistic strivings to be a writer kept her isolated. She defended her loneliness as an effort not to spoil creative inspiration and saw her isolation as the only way to self-actualization.

Victims of trauma especially may need to remain independent of others as a way of remaining safe from more potential hurt. It is very difficult and sometimes impossible to let others in because these victims have been emotionally exploited and taken advantage of in the past. They need to protect themselves in order to preserve a sense of self. Learning to let others in will be a long and thorny path for many of them. It´s important to try to understand that need for self-protection when negotiating all aspects of a relationship.

Ambivalence and Commitment

Ambivalence is commonly defined as having two or more conflicting feelings at the same time, which for many people is hard to tolerate. In its most innocent form it can come across as simple indecisiveness in a day-to-day matter, like having too many choices. After the wall between Eastern and Western Germany came down, one of my friends from the former East used to tell the story of how he first entered a Western supermarket with its abundance of goods. He had planned to buy tomatoes for dinner and was not prepared for the great variety of vegetables that stared at him in the produce section. "There were cherry tomatoes, big beef tomatoes, Florida tomatoes, green tomatoes... I just wanted tomatoes!" He ended up leaving the store, overwhelmed and frustrated, without tomatoes.

The very same dynamic can occur on the job or in the family. I have worked with people who were constantly torn apart by the opposing demands different family members placed on them, always placating everyone without being able to take a breath and think about their own needs. Others are in the throes of obligations and expectations at their workplace, racing back and forth between offices and squeezing in another phone call, and then complaining about how they never have time to think about their own projects. It is not uncommon for them to be told they suffer from attention deficit disorder (ADD) because of their apparent inability to focus on one thing. In reality, it's not that they can't concentrate on a particular task, but that it's impossible to fend off other people's demands. And because they can rarely say no, the same people will come back repeatedly to try to dump on them.

For some people, choosing a girlfriend or a husband can become one's personal inter-relational tomato overload. "But what if someone better comes along" is a thought that plagues many gentle narcissists when they are confronted with the demand or the desire to commit to a partner. They feel ambivalent about everything, from their boyfriend's choice in clothes or their girlfriend's parents, sometimes even whether they want to have children with this person.

But ambivalence is more than just an annoying inability to say no or to make decisions. We can also use our familiarity with ambivalence to understand the many nuances that color human experience. Our Western culture tends to put a lot of emphasis on mastering our feelings and quickly coming to a decision between either/or. But human behavior is more than making a rational choice about a task at hand. It is about navigating relationships in the personal, professional and institutional realms. We are all embedded in a greater context of family, friends, colleagues, institutions, societies and cultures. All of these have a certain influence on us, and the combined impact of these relationships, together with the memory of our own previous experiences, form a person's decision-making process, and many times those influences contradict each other.

Ambivalent feelings are present in our most important relationships from the minute we are born. We may love our parents deeply, and yet they can drive us crazy in any aspect of daily life. As children, we may love the warmth and safety of sitting in mother's lap but hate our dependency on her. We may harbor gnawing feelings of rivalry towards our siblings and still adore them for their competence and guidance. We can have love-hate relationships with our partners and lovers and still feel unable to fully commit to or separate from them. Why is it that we expect our romantic relationships to be perfect, when nothing like that was true in any other relationship we ever had?

Ambivalence is not a fun feeling to have. We are bewildered and disoriented and we want to get rid of these emotions. What usually provides some kind of relief is the exploration of all these conflicting feelings. The more we become aware of what tortures us, the clearer we tend to become on what we are leaning towards. In therapy we start nurturing these seedlings of what is to become the gentle self's own point of view, as opposed to everybody else´s. What it takes in the meantime is a certain ability to tolerate that feeling of not-knowing-quite-yet what we want. We would rather plunge into action or an activity to distract ourselves from the pain of being ambivalent, or make a quick decision just to get rid of the feeling of being stuck. "Ambivalence is often viewed negatively and is experienced as unpleasant or even painful, yet it often presents an opportunity for growth and change because it involves coming to terms with the rich complexity of experience that might otherwise be avoided and remain hidden in the background," writes the phenomenologist Steve Harris.

President Barack Obama reflected on this briefly while campaigning for office. "There is a certain ambivalence in my character that I like about myself," he told his aides, as quoted in *Newsweek*. "It´s part of what makes me a good writer. It´s not necessarily useful in a presidential campaign." What he expresses is a common dynamic: Ambivalence feels expansive, enriches thought and fantasy, and can be a powerful part of our emotional and intellectual process, but it can equally hamper making an actual decision. Yet the more we learn to tolerate ambivalence and just leave ourselves alone, the more naturally we will come to decide on a course of action, because it will also make it easier to tolerate perhaps having made the wrong decision. The key, as always, is to find the right balance between being able to tolerate ambivalence and just taking the plunge and making a decision, all the while risking the possibility of going the wrong way.

Even though we tend to experience our ambivalence as a burden, it comes with one clear advantage: the ability to put ourselves into another person's shoes, the capability of real empathy, which is what makes compromise and human relationships possible. Yet again, as soon as we see things from a different perspective, an easy resolution becomes more and more difficult, and any attempt at returning to simplistic black-and-white thinking is futile. We start to see things the way they really are, in all their imperfections, instead of insisting on our own one-dimensional perspective. That in turn enables us to negotiate an agreement with our partners and colleagues.

Stubbornly insisting on our single-minded point of view usually doesn't get us very far. Maturity is about finding a consensus with which everyone who is involved can be happy, not steamrolling our way to our egocentric goals. Wisdom is the capacity to see your own limitations and try to come to terms with it.

Finding a consensus usually involves conflict. We are afraid of conflict because in the past, more often than not, we lost the argument. Worse, sometimes we lost the person we wanted to be with. Loss is a powerful motivator to give up our own position. We would rather give in quickly in order to get rid of the tension. But conflict can be a rich source of expansion if we make it part of our inner dialogue. Of course, this is a fairly abstract thought. Nobody likes to experience the pain of conflict. But pain is the great equalizer. Everybody is in pain at times. It makes us feel compassionate with those who go through it. It renders all symbols of power and influence meaningless. And it makes us appreciate the times without it a lot more.

Loneliness

Although many gentle selves feel uneasy in certain social settings, at the same time we often dread being alone. Many of us experience a fear of disaster when we are lonely, a fear that something could happen to us: we might have a heart attack or an accident, or someone could rob or kill us. Forced to be alone, we don't know what to do with ourselves; we get anxious and antsy and crave distraction in order to escape the growing fear of being thrown back onto ourselves. We often stay in unhappy relationships far too long out of fear of being alone or of not finding another partner ever again. We need safety from being abandoned and yet don´t feel quite able to fully engage with one another.

What´s lacking is a cohesive sense of self that prevents or at least contains the anxiety that comes up when feeling lonely. Kohut called these personalities "merger hungry": we crave to merge psychologically with an idealized other who can support and comfort our fragile self. Being able to depend on others, to ask for what is needed, being a part of a greater community is a sign of maturity. It helps us look beyond our self centered, narcissistic point of view and enables us to give to others. Yet the melting into a larger entity can also lead to an extreme state, when the self is obliterated and dependent solely on outside support. We need to develop a certain capacity to be alone with ourselves and to have trust in the world around us, which makes possible the belief that we won´t be let down when we fall on hard times. We become able to truly enjoy being by ourselves.

This is when loneliness turns into a solitude that can be fully appreciated. It occurs when we feel one with our surroundings, and it is easiest appreciated when we are in nature. It is in the mountains and by the sea that we can fully enjoy the vastness of life, which makes our inner self expansive and restful and provides us with the "oceanic feeling" that even Sigmund Freud talked about. The fear of being lonely is of course more than understandable in this world of give and take. We are horrified by newspaper accounts of elderly people dying alone and not being found for days or even months. But there is a middle way between isolation and a fear of connection and losing the self by clinging to the other.

To some extent, loneliness is a state of mind: When we are alone, we feel anxious and afraid of neglect or abandonment. Part of that fear makes us want to shut down and shut out the world around us. We separate from the sounds and voices of our surroundings and retreat into our inner lives, which are too fragile to sustain a feeling of connectedness with the larger world. As soon as we reengage, whether it is with a close friend or a stranger or even just the stimuli of our immediate surroundings, we reconnect and become a part of a larger perspective. "We lose ourselves in ourselves," writes political scientist Thomas Dumm. "It is an experience composed of a loss of the capacity to experience."

Many studies have shown that we need other people in order to survive psychologically. From the very beginnings of Homo sapiens, we have been a tribal species that could not make it against the threats of the outside world without teaming up with others and finding a consensus about how to proceed. Studies have shown that when left alone, we tend to soothe our fears with too much alcohol or unhealthy food, we exercise less, have less fun and vegetate alone in front of the TV. It even impacts our physical health, increasing the production of stress hormones and having a negative effect on our immune and cardiovascular systems. And while there is nothing wrong with relaxing while watching your favorite series, it is, again, about balance. If all we do is watch TV and don´t get out of the house at all, chances are something isn´t right. The same goes for so-called compulsive sociability, when the inability to be alone manifests itself in an unceasing need to be involved in social activities which often end up involving more mindless chatter than meaningful interpersonal connection.

Many people spent a good part of the day alone when they were children. Even when they were around siblings and family, they may not have been truly engaged with them. For them, solitude is often ingrained in their personalities and they have learned to be completely independent. For them, the journey is about finding a healthy balance between "going it alone" and being with others, letting other people in. There is nothing wrong with craving solitude and independence. It is all about finding the right social environment of like-minded people who seek the same level of closeness and distance, and where you can be yourself.

Decision-making

Sometimes one of the hardest things to do is make decisions. Where am I going to live? Which school will I pick? Where do I buy a house? How do I raise my kids? Should I stay with my partner or leave? These are questions many have difficulty deciding for themselves. We become attached to what we have and it is hard to imagine what it will be like when we strive for more. We don´t feel strong enough to tackle a new life, and it seems safer to suffer quietly with the circumstances we've settled into than to take a risk and go after a goal that seems out of reach. We are afraid we are setting ourselves up for failure and cling to what we have.

Many gentle narcissists agonize greatly over a decision about when to take the step to make a change in their lives. It often feels like too great a risk to pursue a new profession or a new relationship if what is desirable seems to be hard to attain. We don´t feel strong enough to pursue the satisfaction of our own needs and often don´t have the support to take action. Sometimes the anxiety is so pervasive that it´s even hard to decide how to go about handling everyday life, whether doing laundry is more important than washing the dishes, or seeing this friend is more pressing than seeing another. We get lost in trying to attain perfection and end up not making a decision at all.

Living with someone who has a hard time making decisions can become a challenge in itself. We are tempted to just tell them what to do and how to go about it, while harsh instructions and an annoyed command to just make a decision will have, if any, the opposite effect. The person criticized in this way feels infantilized and pushed around and will shut down rather than take the well-meant advice.

Especially when it comes to making a commitment, many take a long time to get to that point because they never feel quite sure if this is what they want. They feel great ambivalence about deciding if they want to forge a bond that is supposed to last a lifetime if they are not convinced of their choice in the first place. Some people end up not marrying at all because of their ambivalence. Others marry three or four times because they are unsure of what they need, and it takes them decades to find out what kind of partner really suits them and who can meet their needs. They usually don't have a malicious plan to seduce and subsequently abandon their partners but suffer from an inability to know what works in the first place and being forced to find out along the way.

Competition

Competition can be hard to deal with for any mortal. Animals are called territorial when they fight another contender that's threatening their livelihood, and executives and athletes need to be competitive in order to be successful. But in relationships competition often triggers jealousy, and we are quickly told to forget our narcissistic instincts and "just get along."

For those gentle narcissists who have suppressed their own desires all their lives, it is a sign of progress when they begin to compete. For those who have made withdrawal deep into the self a pervasive way of coping and waive any opportunity to take the stage, even having feelings of jealousy is a sign that something is changing in their attitude about themselves. As children we learned to give in to whatever the dominant person in the family demanded, often without questioning. Maybe we tried to stand up and get some unbiased attention at a very young age but remained without response and support, or we were beaten into submission without getting a chance to recover. Some of us may not even have engaged in any kind of sibling rivalry by immediately handing over to the more dominant sibling the right to express ourselves or ask for anything. Once we begin to feel jealous and start demanding attention, we have begun to break out of our cocoons and engage with the world.

The first arena where we compare ourselves to others is the family. When the caregiver can´t pay attention in a meaningful way, the child may surrender any desire for it. Even having a parent who is very anxious and insecure and constantly worries about the child without conveying a sense of strength and agency can do a lot of damage. The anxiety a mother feels may become so overwhelming that all she does is question her own abilities. In a way she is constantly preoccupied with herself and has no capacity to really feel what the child needs, even though she fusses relentlessly. If an insecure mother has to deal with a "problem child" and spends all her energy taking care of this child's needs, she withdraws her attention from a generally healthy sibling, who then automatically feels that she has no right to demand more attention. Any sense of indignation she might have is repressed in the service of the sibling, who seemingly has a greater need to be taken care of.

For many, competition is a constant, torturous reminder of their struggle to compare themselves to others. A new boyfriend may wonder if his predecessor was making more money or performed better sexually, while a newly minted wife might worry if she is as attractive or outgoing as her sister-in-law. In the family we tend to compete for the attention of the parents, in-laws and older siblings; at work it is for the attention of the one in charge. We want to come off as superior to others and leave the insufferable rivals in the dust. It's a lifelong struggle to overcome our narcissi̶t̶i̶c̶ ̶d̶e̶s̶i̶r̶e̶ to be the best and brightest, and to dev̶e̶l̶o̶p̶ generosity to acknowledge that the needs̶ ̶o̶f̶ ̶t̶h̶e̶ other are as equally legitimate as one's own. ̶A̶l̶l̶ ̶w̶e̶ can do is create awareness and good judgment about when we need to put the self first and when the other.

5. The Path to Healing

Expanding the Lost Self

Narcissism is not just a pathological character trait. It also means self-love. It's a vital part of existence and the reason we want to live. In a way, we are all narcissists, it just depends on whether it´s beyond the normal need to be paid attention to. Narcissism is at work when we look for a partner, raise our children to be the way we'd like them to be, and look for professional or spiritual goals to achieve a meaningful life. There *is* healthy narcissism. Unfortunately, narcissism has gotten a bad reputation and is used today primarily to characterize the self-involved, the selfish, those who are just no fun to be around because everything's always about them.

It's undeniable that we all want to be special in our own way. We want people to laugh at our jokes and respond to our comments. We want and need attention. In fact, we want to be unique and original in just about everything we do, whether it's the way we raise our children or decorate our homes. We want to have an impact and make a difference while we're on this earth—and leave a legacy after we´re gone. Most of all, we want to be special to our romantic partners and our children. Sadly, with our community engagement in decline and our friendships challenged by the pressures of daily life, we tend to overburden our immediate families with our expectations of unconditional love and never-ending romance, which is partly why so many of our relationships fail.

Gentle selves, too, have narcissistic issues because they seemingly give up their self-love in service to others. And while this sounds like a laudable quality that in fact could be used by any religion to embody the ideal of selflessness and surrender, in reality there is no such thing — or at least very rarely — as the complete giving up of one's own self-centered way of thinking for the benefit of others.

If we are truly honest with ourselves, most of our actions and emotions are motivated by some kind of self-interest. Especially if we grow up with all sorts of religious ideals, it may be tempting to keep a tab on all the things we do to be good. We develop a whole strategy of how to live up to a religious rule that was usually set forth by the family saint. *If I go to the temple every week — even if I don't have to — grandma will give me a treat. If mother doesn't notice how I say an extra prayer, then God sure does.* And so it goes throughout adult life: *If I donate a couple of dollars to this cause I am still a good person, even if I don't travel to Bangladesh to help the flood victims there. If I help out my colleague with the sick kid she might do he same for me.* Of course, some good deeds are performed from purely altruistic motives. Most of the time, though, there are other reasons that have a lot more to do with give-and-take and tit-for-tat. Contemplative practices like meditation provide a great opportunity to learn more about ourselves in that way. As soon as we take a good look at what really goes on in our minds throughout the day, we see there isn't usually much thinking about how to serve others. It's about our very own interests and self-perception. We will come back to this in a later chapter on meditation.

Despite our self-absorption, it so often proves to be impossible for gentle narcissists to translate the self-centered nature of our thoughts into looking out for ourselves in the daily struggle for love and attention. We tend to step back modestly when praise is showered upon the collective at a family gathering. We don't complain when a raise goes to a coworker and not to us. We stay in the background when a leader is needed, even if no one else has the skills required, many times simply because we don't want to appear arrogant or self-important. I don't mean to suggest that we should all turn into egotists and brag about our achievements. But there is a middle ground that allows us to feel good about ourselves and still watch out for others in the process.

Many gentle narcissists torture themselves with such self-defeating thoughts as "the people in Africa have it so much worse than I do." They have trouble acknowledging their own suffering and put other peoples' perspectives first. While thinking about the less privileged in the world is an honorable thing that reminds us of our interconnectedness, feeling bad about ourselves isn't going to do a thing for anyone. We can be a lot more effective by containing whatever resentment we may have for the people around us and take care of the relationships we have.

Self-esteem is nurtured in early childhood, when the infant is still absorbed by a developmentally appropriate, natural grandiosity — or "expansiveness," as some call it. In the infant's mind, only she and the mother — and later the father or any equivalent — exist, and everything that goes on revolves around her. What the baby, and later the child, needs during this time is for her actions and initiatives to be enjoyed and mirrored back by the parents' well-meaning responses. By "mirroring" we mean simply reflecting back what was communicated, as a signal that we understand the child wants to be known and validated: *Oh, you hurt your knee!* or *I know you love Elmo,* or, slightly more sophisticated, *So, you want to know why the sky is blue?* If such mirroring does not occur on a consistent basis all the joy about being alive and being in the world, as well as a sense of empowerment and agency, are suppressed.

Neuroscience has been assisting psychoanalysis in this approach, and the so-called mirror neurons have gotten a lot of positive coverage lately. Mirror neurons are a class of brain cell that provides the basis of social behavior. A number of recent studies have shown that mirror neurons are at work when we imitate the gestures or actions of others (like scratching one's head when someone else does), and more importantly, when we feel empathy with them. They fire away when we see what others have (which ranges from a simple *I want ice cream, too!* to a complex *I wish I were in a committed relationship as well*), when we spontaneously react with the same gesture to someone waving at us (or flipping us the bird), or join another voluntary helper when someone collapses right in front of us. The existence of mirror neurons explains why we tend to conform with the majority in a group, or why we get turned on by watching a couple make love. They even make us do things we would never have expected were in us, when someone else leads the way. Mirror neurons have been found to form the basis for social interaction and human relatedness altogether.

Because there often was or still is a lack of mirroring for the gentle self, she can often literally *not see herself*. She is unaware that others want her attention and her opinion and prefers to hide in the background. She is disconnected from her body, often doesn´t want to showcase it and hides it under a cloak of baggy clothes and modest colors. A simple trick to create more self awareness is simply to put up more mirrors in the house. Notice yourself. See for yourself who you are. Watch your position in a group of family members or friends in the mirror to create a better understanding of what you are doing. It might surprise you.

Many gentle narcissists have a hard time accepting how much we depend on other people's influence, even though this dynamic exists in virtually every person. They blame themselves for being weak after having agreed to a group decision they secretly might have second thoughts about. They worry that they should have made their point in an argument a lot more decisively out of fear of looking like a pushover. They feel resistant about courting another person, because the object of their desire should be making his own decision without being persuaded or influenced in any way, or because they secretly want to be courted themselves. They notoriously underestimate their own power over others, deeply convinced that they will never be able to change anybody's mind.

The truth is that we all are *inherently impressionable*, differently so at different times and by different people, but still adaptable in order to adjust and become integrated into whatever social situation we find ourselves in. And although it is culturally not necessarily a desirable quality, changing your mind is something that happens naturally and constantly, depending on who or what you are influenced by and who in your immediate environment has just changed his mind. Whether we take advantage of it or not, we were made to live as social beings who affect one another, which explains why we suffer when we feel left out or can't get ourselves to participate.

The dynamic that we are who we hang out with has been confirmed by many studies. Some people, for example, become overweight if they surround themselves with other overweight people because their physical shape is tolerated in this group. People who seek out friends who are happy and content with their lives are on average happier themselves. The term "infectious laughter" is no random invention. We love to join a person who is happy because it makes us happy in return. We are made to connect and bond with each other, and our lives are intricately interconnected, sometimes into death. Many years ago, I knew an elderly couple that had been married for over fifty years. When the husband died unexpectedly, his wife developed a number of new health problems, and within a few weeks she passed away as well.

Of course the same dynamic can backfire just as forcefully. When, in 2008, onetime presidential candidate John Edwards admitted that he'd had an affair while campaigning, he defended himself, saying: "In the course of several campaigns I started to believe that I was special and became increasingly egocentric and narcissistic." His conviction of "being special" in this instance most likely arose when countless enthusiastic admirers projected their idealized image of perfection and power onto him. Like so many other celebrities before him who couldn't handle the great amount of public adoration, he started to believe the idealized version of what other people saw in him, became grandiose and deluded himself into thinking he was invincible to being found out.

The same "infectious" social dynamic unfolds when we live in an emotionally toxic environment. Bitterly narcissistic families in which no one is capable of paying attention to anyone but themselves create deprived and emotionally starved children. And if it is impossible to find an environment that is more positive and supportive, they themselves may very well procreate another generation of emotionally unavailable and enfeebled children.

Yet somewhere in us there is the desire to break out of this cycle of deprivation and hopelessness. We feel we need to get away from the hurt and the negativity and build something better for ourselves. But how? Because gentle narcissists feel so powerless and at the same time often have a strong instinct to get out of a harmful or uninspiring environment, they tend to feel drawn to people they can idealize for their strength, achievement and determination. Sometimes this hopeful tendency is buried under an expectation of the self to remain independent—so independent that it seems impossible to admire anyone, because the need to be emotionally self-sufficient is so great. But even if it is not immediately accessible, most of us do have a desire to find a role model we can live up to, who inspires us to want more and to live a more engaged and fulfilling life. Some admire a celebrity or an outstanding intellectual, which can be motivating but also overwhelming, because it easily starts to feel as if we will never get there, and then the admiration turns into something discouraging and hopeless. A lot more useful is a person whom we can talk to, who gives something back and takes on a supportive function by offering positive feedback to what we have to bring to the table.

What is needed, is a greater attention to our own *expansiveness*, a term that was proposed by the psychoanalysts Stolorow and Atwood. Gentle narcissists, who have never learned how to channel their normal expansiveness in childhood into healthy self-esteem and always hold themselves back, need to learn how to revive and enlarge this greater sense of self that is lying dormant within them. They need to stop being small and get comfortable with trying to shine. We all need sources that make us feel good about ourselves so that we can give to others. Nobody can run on a battery without having it recharged frequently.

Whoever can be a mentor to you—or simply supports you in your strivings—should be kept close. You don't have to feel held hostage by the bad experiences of childhood, because all the relationships in our lives have an effect on us throughout our development, although it has to be admitted that those in our formative years tend to lay the groundwork for our relational capacities. Yet it's never too late to surround yourself with positive and supportive people who encourage your endeavors and give well-intended feedback.

The most important goal to improve the life of a chronically depleted and potentially depressed person is to give them room to expand: to explore their innate talents and creativity, their skills and beliefs. Be persistent. Create awareness of your own personality by meditation or working with a coach or a psychotherapist. Train your mind to pay attention to yourself and others on a regular basis. Just like we work out the body, we need to keep our minds sharp and aware. The brain is quite able to adjust to new circumstances and a new, more positive environment. Studies have shown that the change is visible not just in our behavior but in our brain waves as well. Nobody achieves a big goal without hard work. Persistence will be rewarded with change.

A form of expansiveness occurs when you start standing up for yourself. It was such a pleasure when one of my clients one day came in and said "I'm tired of eating shit," and his usually resigned look took on an air of spite. He had been getting up all night to take care of his sick child, and his wife had ordered him around one too many times. He was ready to strike back. He was angry but tired and so worn out physically and emotionally that the swing he wanted to take at her resembled more the nudge of a cat who wants to play. He wanted to stand up to her and to everybody else in the process who had made him "eat shit" all his life. But he didn't have the grand revolution in him. Instead, he let the opportunity pass, made a note in his mind and waited for the next occasion, yet another time when he would have to do the dirty work. The time came and instead of just giving in, he gathered all his strength and said no. He didn't sneer, he didn't squirm. He simply did nothing but hold his ground. He weathered his wife's loud and intimidating yelling attack, he didn't engage in a screaming match and he didn't walk out of the room in silent desperation. He just stood there and waited for the storm to pass. And it did. He had finally stood up for himself.

Dealing with Unpleasant Feelings

Part of the gentle narcissists's innate tendency to withdraw stems from the inability to tolerate a certain amount of anxiety or other forms of discomfort. When an argument with a partner gets too heated, walking away often becomes the number one defense mechanism. Even love and affection are sometimes hard to take. Tender feelings and vulnerability are difficult to own up to, let alone share them with your partner. It´s important that we try to develop the capacity to hold difficult emotions without acting on them. The ability to contain enables us to fully experience intense situations without giving in to the automatic urge to leave or burst out in anger or distract ourselves with the entertainment of the day. This is especially true for more severe forms of avoidance and escapism like alcoholism, drugs, gambling or any other form of addictive behavior.

An ongoing introspective practice like meditation or psychotherapy enables us to be more aware of just holding still for a second in the space between feeling an intense emotion and wanting to do something about it. If we can just be still for that moment we have more control over deciding what we actually want to do, for example, whether we want to turn away or yell back at somebody who hurt us.

If you feel strong anxiety or pain or even a nervous breakdown approaching, the first rule to remember is: leave yourself alone. We often tend to put more pressure on ourselves in the form of "I can´t possibly burst into tears right now," "what´s wrong with me" or "I hate myself." Instead of being self-critical be your own friend when others make your life difficult and try to stop judging yourself. Make an attempt to empathize with your more fragile self: Of course I feel tired and vulnerable after running around like a madman all day. Of course I get angry when people don´t respond to me, because that´s been the pattern throughout my life.

Gentle people are often receivers, the so called "yin" types in Chinese medicine. We are the ones who listen, who nurture, who accommodate and comfort and try to contain other people's distress. But too much self-containment can be harmful too. There needs to be an outlet for the gentle self to have the chance to have his own stress relieved. If we don't take care of ourselves, our frustration and disappointment with life's pitfalls will come out in passive-aggressive gestures. When anger becomes overwhelming, it's good to be able to contain these negative emotions, in order to prevent the harmful chain reactions of destructive behavior.

One way to gain more control in these situations is simply to imagine what it would be like when two partners fall into the same argument for the thousandth time. Instead of bickering about why the dishes are not done, there could be a conversation about how overloaded your spouse feels when he comes home at night. Or you could do the dishes without saying a word. And maybe next time, he'll do them voluntarily. Or there could be an open dialogue about how overwhelmed you feel. As soon as we take a step back and take a moment to think, we have more control over our actions and those of the people around us.

One of my clients, a middle-aged man named Garry, started therapy in conjunction with meditation practice. He had complained about having a short temper and lashing out at his wife when he was stressed, even if she had nothing to do with his bad mood. The intense introspection enabled Garry gradually to become aware of his feelings. He realized that he had felt all his life that no one had really paid attention to him so that now when someone was absentminded or simply didn´t hear him, he got angry very quickly and blamed it on the other person. The self-exploration he engaged in gradually helped him to contain his anger and fear of being overlooked again, in a way that enabled him not to get caught in his usual destructive behavior. He quickly noticed when he was about to lash out and simply turned away from the stressful situation. Instead he started to focus on what was happening moment to moment, so he could let go of his feelings of anger and just focus on the task at hand. He gained control over his behavior and was able to improve his relationships with his wife and family.

Finding and Being with a Mate

Gentle narcissists crave seeing themselves in the other: we want to have friends and partners who know exactly how we feel about ourselves and others — what it means to us to hold a certain profession, how it feels to be hurt or rejected. We rightfully want to be included when a decision is made that concerns us. We want to be understood even when we make irrational decisions, want to be able to show off what we know and be admired for our skill. When we feel overwhelmed, we want to be taken by the hand and comforted and cared for and be able to trust the other without having to worry about it going wrong.

In our modern world, the demands on the romantic partner seem to increase more and more. We want our partners and spouses to understand us and be there for us and for them to pay attention to our needs. We want them to be attuned to our emotional states and mirror our own preferences and behaviors. We want to be able to admire them for something they have achieved, and be admired in return for what we bring to the table. Of course, there are certain non-negotiables in a relationship, and it's good to know what they are. If your first husband never wanted to have sex and the lack of intimacy ruined your marriage, it's a good idea to pay attention to this next time around. But we have to accept that it's impossible for all of these needs to be met at all times. We need to learn how to deal with being frustrated in that regard without allowing the relationship to become dull and unsatisfying. There is a middle ground between communicating what you need and coming to terms with the limitations of your partner.

Many people complain about the lack of romance and sexual connection in a long-term relationship. It's hard for them to express their dissatisfaction or to ask to spice things up a bit. It feels like romance should be spontaneous, something the partner should just know about the other without having to plan or verbally address it. But it's not a meaningless platitude that relationships are work. And this is a time when effort is required. If we are lazy and don't try to infuse new and exciting experiences into our relationship, it will start to feel stale and boring, and it won't be long before one of the two of us wants out.

Sometimes, though, the connection is easily established just by the matching of personality styles. Those who feel that their innate talents and creativity were never fully seen by the world will find it particularly healing when they can be with someone who is interested in just that side of them. When a shy woman, for example, has an interest in art and finds a partner who is fascinated by that topic without needing to compete with her skill or knowledge, it will help her find fulfillment not just in her interest but also in her relationship. If, in return, he is someone who is skilled at making social connections, something she may be lacking, they complement each other. It is important that both try to engage each other in a supportive way, rather than getting impatient about what each of them is lacking.

Gentle narcissists, whose relationships tend to remain on the surface for fear of intimacy, are especially in need of an understanding partner who has the skill and patience to withstand their attempts to create distance and is secure enough to reach out to them and repair what was broken. As soon as a partner is able to accept and help expand that neglected side of them and breathe new life into it, a strong bond is formed.

Because gentle narcissists do long to be mirrored and look for someone they can idealize in certain respects, they often do well in relationships with people who have the same interests, are genuinely supportive and have the strength to tolerate their sensibilities. When they team up with people that are too much like them, they can often end up in dead-end relationships: two ambivalent, withdrawn people who are stuck together, with neither one of them being able make any decisions because they always look for the other person's opinion, will drive each other mad. As Kohut has said, in relationships, only one person gets to act crazy at a time.

Many times, gentle narcissists will remain in relationships that are no longer tolerable, but they are so afraid of being alone that they won´t risk a breakup. Sometimes they move from one relationship to the next very quickly and feel comfortable leaving a partner only when a new one is already standing by, which makes affairs — that may or may not lead to a new relationship — such a common occurrence.

A similar dynamic is often present with friends: although aware that their circle of friends isn´t supportive, many people will hold on to them for fear of having no one to turn to at all. Yet having supportive social ties is the most crucial ingredient in the gentle self´s psychological recovery and throughout life: we need people who support our strivings without wanting to dominate our decisions, but have the courage to intervene when we go too far astray and turn to destructive behaviors. If you are feeling fragile and lacking a sense of control, it can be balanced by surrounding yourself with people who display a certain strength, serve as role models and are willing to help you out where you need it. But this constellation too can turn to an extreme. People who prove to be too strong and stubborn can become overbearing and may make you feel paralyzed and stifled. It is important to learn for yourself what degree of input and support feels right for you. Only you will know how to balance your needs with what others have to offer.

Connection, Connection, Connection

Humans are by nature intensely social beings. We feel better when we know there is a family to fall back on in case things go awry. We feel comforted when we can talk to a friend when we are lonely. It's soothing to know that there are other people on the subway in the middle of the night. Someone who is isolated will gladly go to the doctor's office just to sit in the waiting room or have five minutes with the physician. No wonder Catholics cherish the idea of having a guardian angel, someone who will always be there when we are about to get ourselves into a foolish situation, hoping that someone, something will prevent us from doing it.

Even a brief encounter with a stranger in the street can feel refreshing and energizing. I remember I was walking down a New York City street one day, deep in thought, when I saw a homeless man standing under an awning of a side street business. When he caught my eye, he spontaneously fell on his knees, put his hands together and cried "Marry me!" I burst into laughter right there, which brought a grin to the man's face, and while I kept on walking, he had cheered me up and the smile on my face lingered for a while. Who knows how many women he had already proposed to that day?

Many studies have shown how important social connections are to our well-being and how they even contribute to our longevity. People who keep close to family or alternatively have a solid circle of friends — or even just one close friend — live longer and healthier lives, are less overweight and are less prone to illness — mentally and physically. It´s long been said that married people are happier than singles. Newer research shows, though, that it´s not being married but simply having connections to the outside world that keeps us alive. It doesn´t matter if you are single or teamed up with a partner or have several children, as long as you can find some way to relate to others that is meaningful to you.

Many gentle narcissists don't have close ties with their families. They feel rejected or burdened by their parents and alienated from their siblings and are in need of an alternative social circle where they feel welcome. Many people choose to cultivate "Wahlverwandschaften" ("elective affinities"), a term made famous by a novel of that name by the German poet Johann Wolfgang von Goethe. It describes the dynamic of how we prefer to team up with people we have a certain chemistry with, rather than feeling forced to nurture relationships that are imposed by societal norms and expectations, like marrying within one's social class and having to get along with the members of the family.

But it's difficult to find a whole new circle of friends when you feel lonely and isolated and disconnected from your peers. When I was in the throes of depression and anxiety after cutting the ties with a community that didn't work for me anymore, I didn't have anyplace to start. I felt shy and fragile and in no position to just go out and make new friends. In the past, I had always been able to pull together individuals whom I met on random occasions to form my own community of like-minded people. But when things fall apart and your confidence is low, it's not easy to start all over again.

Around that time I stumbled upon a Buddhist meditation group. I had begun to read about Zen, and was fascinated by the thought of being able to free yourself from the shackles of your own self-centeredness. Entering a new group was no easy task. I'm not sure what was worse — the impression that some of the people seemed to know each other for years and had long, pre-established relationships, which made it hard to join in, or the sense of disconnect that lingered over the place as a whole, where a seemingly ever-changing group of people came together and then fell apart again, not knowing if I would see them again. What kept me coming back was the attachment to the teacher, who seemed to have a lot to give and a lot to teach. The relationship with him became the first connection, and maybe other members of the community felt the same way and started to come back more regularly. Over time all my other ties to the community would be built upon this first connection to the teacher. It made me stick around, rather than quickly turn away and look for another community that may or may not have made me feel more welcome. The teacher, and gradually members of the group as well, provided me with the stability and encouragement I needed to commit to the community. I was able to grow roots there and it became an integral part of my life. Give yourself the time you need to connect, be patient with yourself and go at a pace that works for you.

Religious groups are not for everyone. There are many other forms of possible connection for the gentle narcissist. We may not have the same habit of making friends as do more outgoing and extroverted people. But that doesn't mean that we can't have other connections that are much more meaningful to us than going to a noisy bar or a crowded party. Because we are capable of listening to the more subtle expressions of life and get easily overwhelmed by too much stimuli, we prefer quieter settings of coming together, like taking a class, joining a discussion group or a book club, or taking the dog for a walk in the park.

When I first started Zen practice, I was bothered by the fact that there was little opportunity to talk to each other. Just sitting silently in a meditation hall without being able to look the other person in the eye seemed like just another form of disconnect. But over the years I started paying attention to the more subtle ways of being around each other, just hearing another person breathe or move — that too is a way of taking the other in, of being present with their embodied being, of knowing them even without putting words to our relatedness.

When we are pensive and in transition, we retreat from the world and are more interested in looking at what is going on inside of ourselves. At these times we have no use for the overwhelming sounds and hectic pace of life. We seek communion with the elements, enjoy walking through the woods or along a beach, and prefer to be around animals rather than people. We fall silent, listen to the sounds of the world, see the rhythm of the seasons in a larger context. We open up to other ways of connecting to a larger world without words, without language, and feel comforted just by watching the changing tides of the sea or the sound of the trees bending in the wind. It doesn't matter how you connect to the world, whether it's finding a mate and having children, taking care of your pets or going out into nature. Even just being around people, living in the city without talking to anybody is a way of connecting to a larger entity.

Connection means different things for different people. Try to accept what works for you and gently push yourself to stick with social situations that may initially feel difficult, if you feel isolated and lonely. We need to be honest about our needs and limitations. With time, we learn how to be a part of a larger community. Give yourself that time.

Connections are made in concentric circles. Right here next to us is our partner — or we would like her to be. Then come children and our family of origin. After that, it's friends, colleagues and community. Just as our closest allies influence us, so do our peers in our immediate surroundings as well as the nation we belong to. And finally, we are citizens of the earth. But it doesn't have to be that way. Many people are happy skipping the first and even the second circle and jumping right to the next. Each of us builds her own network of circles, and what that looks like is entirely up to you.

Culture plays a role in all of this. If we don't feel accepted by or integrated into our culture — be it work culture or the geographical region you live in — it will come out in our emotional well-being. We don't feel accepted and understood and become outsiders. But there are many ways to feel part of a culture. Some people replace it with the word tribe: the larger context we want or don't want to belong to — the profession we choose, the neighborhood we live in, the sports team we root for. We call ourselves New Yorkers or Catholics, Yankee fans, anthropologists or housewives, runners, environmentalists, computer nerds, Toastmasters or jazz fans. Even if we feel isolated, there is still a group we have grown up with or grown into. These communities have an enormous impact on us. It's all about finding the culture or tribe that suits you, where you feel at home and that makes you feel stronger because you have the backing of the group.

In some cultures, the individual perspective will always move into the background in favor of the group. After the devastating tsunami in Japan in 2011 and the ensuing nuclear threat that came from the damaged power plant in Fukushima, the Japanese came together. They gathered their belongings and looked out for each other. The world came to them. Similarly, in the aftermath of September 11, 2001, in New York City, for a brief moment in time New Yorkers looked at each other with non-discriminating empathy. Nobody was excluded. We were all going through the same thing. Nobody refused to help.

Certain societies will always put the interests of the group first. When an achievement has been accomplished, it shines on the whole tribe. If one of its members brings shame to it, the group as a whole will suffer. But in an individualized culture like the U.S., where every single person fights for himself and accordingly reaps the benefits of his success, submitting to a greater social entity isn't the norm and can carry a certain stigma. This dynamic can lead to great conflicts between partners from different cultural backgrounds. A couple with roots in Southeast Asia I once worked with was constantly on the verge of a breakup, because in his family the younger generations automatically submitted to the will of the older relatives, while her family members related to each other in equal terms and children frequently spoke out against their elders in search of meeting their own needs.

Cultural influences can dominate the way we look at how to deal with our narcissism. Growing up in Germany in the 1960s and 1970s, I never heard very much talk about being special or unique. It was about obligation, loyalty and commitment to your partner, as well as to the community — ironically not so much to the family. The post-war generational split, between the older segments of the population, which were mostly caught up in how not to deal with their personal conduct during the Nazi era, and the increasingly inquisitive generations that were to follow, ran straight through millions of families and led to at least some degree of alienation between parents and children. In many social entities there is a similar ongoing debate and sometimes a conflict between individual desire and the traditional social order.

In the U.S., wanting to be special or unique to others is a lifelong quest that is very openly pursued and reflected upon. That is not to say that individuals in other cultures don't grapple with it. While I was growing up, the narcissistic needs of every individual — although rarely openly addressed — were very much a driving force in daily behavior. But rather than putting them out into the world for people to respond to, they were mostly repressed, only to surface in other less direct ways. In many cultures whose members don't admit openly to their narcissistic needs the way many Americans do, those needs are at least partially repressed. Other needs, though, will be met through the larger contexts of family, community and society.

One example is the book *Battle Cry of the Tiger Mother*, written by a Chinese-American mother of two young daughters, in which a rigorous education without any coddling or spoiling is promoted. To me it seems that the mother's own unmet needs have been projected onto her daughters. Whatever she wasn't able to receive that she needed from her own caretakers and that may have gotten lost in the almost culturally manifested striving for perfection, needed to be recovered by raising her daughters to be perfect children so that she could shine in their glory. Her potentially repressed desire for attention was thus compensated for by displacing it onto her children. The jury is still out on how these two girls perceived their upbringing. Sooner or later, we will hear their accounts.

Role Models

Gentle narcissists thrive when we have role models to look up to and hold on to. We all are inherently social beings and compare ourselves with the people surrounding us. Some people have a hard time accepting this about themselves. "I should be more independent" is a common complaint. "I shouldn't care so much about what others are thinking." And while our subjective feeling of our own exaggerated malleability may be legitimate, a part of us will always look outside to see what the rest of the family or our colleagues or the people on the planet are doing.

The most important role models we have are our parents. But it´s not just up to our early role models. We are not doomed by the shortcomings of our early caregivers. We can find them throughout our lives. For some teenagers their coach takes on an important role, or a teacher they admire. Movies like *Dead Poets Society* and *Mona Lisa Smile* feature strong teachers who stand up to the restrictive culture of their respective schools and become loved and admired by their students. For others, it´s the priest or the family doctor or a well-meaning boss. Even a friend whose strength or guidance we admire can be a source of positive feedback and inspiration. The more sources like these we have to draw on, the more opportunities there are to grow. The gentle self with her fragile inner self particularly craves a strong role model — someone who protects her, inspires her, supports her, listens and understands her. She wants to identify with someone who is unafraid and able to confront injustice.

According to self psychological theory, the gentle self craves to merge with an idealized other to absorb some of that strength and to become more powerful and influential. This is part of why beauty and power so often seem to be the perfect match: the powerful business leader who wants to bask in the glory of being with an attractive woman who every other man will admire him for, while she might have been looking for a strong father figure to protect and take care of her. Sometimes this association with something powerful can extend to nature as well, as with the carefree teenager whose hobby is to chase storms, all the while confronting his fear of being destroyed by them. Some people will watch horror movies or gawk at the scene of a car accident. Unconsciously, they are staring down their fear of death by facing disaster directly and seemingly unfazed.

For the gentle narcissist, looking for the right role model may become a challenge. A former client of mine went about this by looking for the right yoga teacher. She purchased a starter pass that allowed her to visit as many classes as she wanted at her local yoga studio for one week. After each lesson she explained to me in great detail what she liked or disliked about each instructor. One was too quiet and aloof, while another made her feel like a baby with her clumsy attempts to praise. Her narrative reminded me of an episode of *Seinfeld*, in which Jerry Seinfeld is having a conversation with his mother. At one point he is asked to open a jar that no one else seems to be able to. When he takes off the lid, his mother claps her hands, singing, "Yay! Jerry got it open!" He just rolls his eyes. It's a classic example of *phase-inappropriate behavior*, as a grown man in his thirties hardly needs to be patted on the back for opening a jar. Equally inappropriate, a yoga instructor can come across this way when teaching a class of adults, when her voice mimics the baby talk of a new mother.

Luckily, that wasn't the end of the story, and she kept looking. One self-deprecating newcomer seemed too insecure to look like he could actually teach anybody anything. Another woman's routine was too strenuous, and her attempts to motivate her students came to feel tyrannical. She eventually ended up with a no-nonsense yet warm and empathic woman who convinced her that she knew what she was doing, and playfully encouraged her to challenge herself without too much pressure. Simply having a role model that communicated strength and commitment served the purpose of inspiring her to keep up her routine and develop a connection to the teacher and the group as well as with her own body. She started to feel more comfortable in her own skin, which became part of developing a greater sense of her whole self.

The same dynamic applies to our vulnerabilities. When our role models can accept and live with their weaknesses, we feel more at ease with our own. TV characters can have a surprising effect in that way. Grace, for example, the red-haired female lead in *Will & Grace*, was really quite a neurotic, clingy and somewhat annoying friend, but she was able to own up to her neuroses and admit when she turned into an obsessive control freak. Similarly, the sneaky and evasive Doug, aka *The King of Queens*, is frequently called out on his cowardice by his loud-mouthed wife Carrie, but after much plotting and arguing they always end up reconciling and accepting each other's flaws. We don't have to put up a tough face and conceal our humanness, because there is nothing wrong with being ourselves.

Awareness

Awareness and *support* are the two components of lasting change and happiness. We must become aware of what we are doing and how our inner world is organized. In addition, in order to live full lives, we need support from people who view us in a positive regard and whom we can trust. Throw in another ingredient that most of us are painfully aware of for its absence: *non-judgment*. When we stop beating ourselves up for all the things we are doing wrong, we can relax and take a better look at the big picture, rather than getting caught up in our own imperfections.

Awareness is essential on our path to healing. Depending on how much you had to defend yourself emotionally against hurt and pain in the past, becoming aware may require a lot of work. If you had to numb yourself in order to survive the pain and criticism inflicted on you, it takes a while to peel back the layers of protective shields. On the contrary, others are already hyperaware of their surroundings but tend to relate to everybody and everything from the vantage point of their anxieties and take even the slightest remark as an attack or a judgment against themselves.

Working on our missing or exaggerated awareness takes time and effort and is really a lifelong learning process. The way I learned to attain a certain degree of awareness was an intense practice of talking about myself in psychoanalysis, and, parallel to that, sitting with my thoughts and feelings in meditation. Both disciplines help immensely in getting to a deeper level of understanding one´s own thoughts and behavior. In Buddhist practice, meditation has been traditionally called the path of awakening. We stop blanking out, avoid the daydreaming and face the realities of life, unfiltered, with all its pain and joy. They say that once you are on that path, you can´t go back. I think you can! If we allow ourselves to fall back into a mental haze or into mind-numbing fear, if we let ourselves be overwhelmed by the difficulties of life without reflecting on them or distract ourselves with the addiction of the day, we will inevitably return to a state of not-so-blissful unawareness.

In our health obsessed culture, people spend a lot of time and money on their physical fitness and also on learning and increasing their mental capacities, but they won´t put much energy into their emotional health. We think that being happy means to have enough money to take care of ourselves and our families, to have fun and be in good physical health. But we don´t learn in school that we need to have well-functioning relationships, and a good relationship is only possible when we have a good relationship with ourselves. Just as the muscles in our bodies need to be worked out in order to be fit, or our fingers have to be exercised in order to play the piano, our mind needs a good workout to be present and connected.

Those of us who have gotten rid of or never had a protective armor and are very sensitive to the stimuli of everyday life are often called empaths — we have antennae for the needs and the suffering of others. Gentle narcissists are sensitive not just in the face of hurt and rejection but also in perceiving the dynamics in their environment. As soon as we allow ourselves to open up to our surroundings and stop repressing our real feelings, a whole world of sensory stimuli washes over us. We are capable of reading other people's body language correctly and have a pronounced ability to catch the vibes, emotions and preconceptions that oscillate between people and that dominate the outcome of how a relationship feels to those who are involved.

Because of this sensitivity, people with our personalities often are, as Fairbairn notes, "capable of greater psychological insight than any other kind of person, due in part to their being so introverted and so familiar with their own deeper psychological process." We can detect another person's hurt just from one glance and have a keen sense of the relational dynamics between others. We can empathize with another person's struggle and can easily see things from a different perspective.

The capacity to be aware and see ourselves from a distance becomes our greatest strength. We start observing ourselves from an outside perspective and begin to realize what we communicate and how we come across to others. Once this awareness starts to form, we gain greater control over what we want from life and how to get it. We are increasingly able to express ourselves freely and enjoy the feeling of having an impact on others.

Psychotherapy

Some of you might feel too depressed or hopeless to muster the motivation to go out and find a positive role model. It's not always that easy. When our inner resources are depleted and our loved ones are absent or feel helpless themselves, we need outside support. In this case a psychotherapist might come in handy, as he or she is available to you in any phase of your development. If you grew up without supportive role models, this connection has the potential to become the first fully developed relationship that can be designed on your own terms, within the boundaries of the profession. The therapeutic relationship can become the template for new and more fully engaged relationships with others. A good therapist should be able to stomach any of your feelings about this relationship, whether it is your impatience with his rigid schedule or feeling hurt about a thoughtless remark he made about you. You should be able to spell out all of your feelings, even if they seem irrational. All these emotions can unfold and be talked about in a safe space without having to be afraid of ridicule, anger or rejection. Every feeling has an origin and has evolved in its own time, and this is what we want to look at closely. And because the same behavioral patterns tend to develop in the relationship with the therapist as in any other relationship, we can use the therapeutic dialogue as an opportunity to talk about it right there if you feel hurt or need to ask for what you need.

Because of our tendency to idealize, the therapist will be molded in our mind to fit this role perfectly.

We admire her composure in the face of difficult emotions, her ability to take a step back and look at them without getting overwhelmed, and many other characteristics that are unique to this person. Many times we feel a twinship or strong identification with her, and we are convinced that she is just like me, that she understands exactly what I am going through because this is what she has already mastered. By directly experiencing how our role model leads the way and seems to take us by the hand, showing us how to do it ourselves, we slowly live up to the strength and experience that in the past we have only admired in others. We become stronger and more confident, and we are able to express our needs directly without the fear of not being heard or misunderstood. This is how our relationships become stronger, too. We are more capable of spelling out our concerns and needs in a calm way, which enables us to start to negotiate with our partners rather than to give in automatically to avoid an argument. We become more involved with the other and can get past our disagreements, which makes our relationships stronger and more fulfilling. It's very much about communication.

The support of the therapist and his understanding of every situation and the feelings that we present is what makes us stronger. We gradually feel less fragile and more courageous in confronting difficult situations. But even though many maladaptive behaviors can be straightened out through therapy, there will always be parts that can't be changed but need to be accepted. A shy, introverted person will not turn into an exuberant extrovert. Instead, she will learn when she can have an impact on others and when to just come to terms with what is already established. She will gain the confidence to be more assertive in some roles and learn how to shrug off unrealistic expectations of herself and others. Equally, our tendency to give in to other people´s decisions will be corrected but not fully eliminated. That is why the gentle self needs to decide carefully where and with whom she wants to get involved. And that is why so many people don´t commit to a new endeavor easily, for fear that they will get sucked into something because they are pushed and not because they are wholeheartedly interested in it.

Psychotherapy is nowadays used for different purposes. Some people just want to get rid of their symptoms, such as anxiety or sadness. Often that is possible in a relatively short period of time, and it matters little whom they work with. Those who are interested in gaining more strength and confidence, though, are better served when they are willing to develop a working relationship with the therapist. And that is when different styles of attachment become interesting.

The most important early thinkers of attachment theory are the British psychoanalysts John Bowlby and the American developmental psychologist Mary Ainsworth. They discovered that when the relationship between the mother and the child is interrupted at an early age, the child will most likely develop one of two attachment styles: "anxious attachment" or "avoidant attachment." Anxiously attached individuals need constantly to be reassured that the relationship is not threatened by abandonment or loss, and they will distrust the stability of each close relationship. Avoidant attachment indicates that the child was rejected, neglected or intruded upon by one or both parents or simply made to feel unwelcome. The individual with this kind of relational style will try not to need anything, to be independent and self-sufficient in order never to be threatened by being rejected again. They have difficulty articulating what they need, expecting to be turned down or disappointed, and often are entirely unaware of their needs. Anxious or avoidant attachment is one of the typical characteristics of the gentle self.

The most important things gentle narcissists learn in therapy or in a close relationship to an idealized teacher or mentor is how to become securely attached and how to articulate frustrations without having to fear loss and rejection. Idealization is sometimes difficult for the gentle narcissist to admit to, because that might mean that they are dependent on another person's opinion and that they are not completely self-sufficient. However, according to Kohut, we all need idealizable role models throughout our lifetime in order to continue to feel supported and actualized. There's nothing wrong with looking for people we want to feel inspired by. Eventually, we will learn that even an idealized role model has flaws. While we grow stronger in our own sense of self, we learn to accept these shortcomings as part of the relationship. We don't need the other person to be perfect anymore and can feel more secure about the give and take of any social system.

Meditation

Meditation has become a widely accepted tool to help calm the mind and learn how to deal with the challenges and stressors of modern life. It has left the realm of organized religion like Zen and Tibetan Buddhism or Christianity and has entered the mainstream without the labels of religious practice that keep many Westerners away. Practices once associated with Buddhist monks or the Dalai Lama, like mindfulness and loving-kindness, have become worthwhile endeavors for all kinds of self-help movements. The world has become smaller. While the West exported its economic principles and its capitalist mantra to the rest of the globe, the East is now penetrating other continents with its religious and philosophical ideals.

The practice of meditation is very simply an ongoing exercise to just be present. Our minds tend to wander off. We like to daydream or worry about things we often have no control over. Many teachers begin by having their students simply focus on the breath while they sit comfortably in a chair or on a cushion. In meditation, we become aware of how hard it is to just pay attention to what is right in front of us. It´s a lot easier to just blank out. Focusing on the breath brings our awareness back to our bodies. We are alive. We breathe. We sit right here. Our thoughts are not reality. That´s all.

Meditation doesn´t mean not thinking. It´s impossible not to think. Thinking is just what the mind does. Instead, we try to become aware and accept the thoughts we have without acting on them. We wear out our worries, our anxiety and our negative beliefs about ourselves. We realize that the same four or five thoughts circle through the mind endlessly. And at one point we are able to distance ourselves from them. The thoughts will still be there but we don´t buy into them the way we used to. Our thoughts are like an annoying uncle who tells the same story over and over and whose narrative becomes a background noise rather than a gripping tale. They are just thoughts. Not reality. The only reality is that we sit here on our chairs and breathe.

Meditation practice has evolved over the years, and since the advent of Zen in America in the last century, new schools of thought have built on the traditional teachings. The practice I originally trained in is the Ordinary Mind School founded by Joko Beck. She taught a form of meditation that focuses on paying attention to one's thoughts, body and the surroundings at the same time. We learn to label our thoughts with words like "worrying," "planning" or "judging" and thus get an idea of what organizes our experience of the world. Most of us are planners. It´s so much more fun to think about tomorrow than to feel the pain or dullness of the present moment. Many of us are worriers. We incessantly worry that something might go wrong. All of us judge. We judge our neighbors and friends, our teachers and peers, and ourselves. The more we become aware of our negative beliefs, our anxiety and fears will move into the background, and we become able to pay attention to our surroundings without neglecting our own needs. At the same time we start to take responsibility for our less flattering behaviors and stand up for ourselves and others.

In the beginning, being with our thoughts might be very scary. We are very much overpowered by the intensity of the fear or anger we are engaged in. All we can do in these initial stages is to let those thoughts and feelings run their course and pass. We might find ourselves in the middle of an argument with an overbearing coworker and feel overwhelmed and helpless. So what do I do in such a situation? Usually there's not much we can do. We will get defensive or even tear up, or we yell back mindlessly. We have no control over our minds. That's just how it will be for a while. But the more we sit and meditate, the less reactive we become. After some time, we might be able to just take a breath before we react, and in that second or two, we have the chance to choose how to respond. It takes time to develop a certain cool in the face of intense feelings. I still get frantic when my ignorant landlord pulls a stunt and tries to tinker with the lease. Some buttons need to be pushed a million times before their mechanics break down. Don't judge yourself while you try to get there.

Once we can let go of our thoughts, a whole new world opens up and we are finally ready to stop and smell the roses. Not only that, we are more open to the spontaneous encounter with another fellow human being—a brief exchange on the subway, in the elevator, at the dog run. For a short moment in time we connect with a stranger. There might be a smile, a dialogue, a considerate gesture and then we move on, going on with our day. We made a connection, and the good vibe that came with it lingers for a while. It made us feel great for a short period of time. It can make your day. Sometimes, whole friendships and relationships start that way.

One of my clients sat for a couple of months, very intensely, sometimes for hours a day when he could. He felt a need to confront himself and the anxiety that pervaded his life. Initially, he had intense feelings of anger and sadness while meditating, but they were not related to any thoughts. He simply sat with intense feelings for months, not knowing what they were about. But slowly some thoughts would break through and he remembered events from his childhood, the trauma of his parents´ divorce and his guilt about leaving his family behind as an adult. At the same time, a muscle tension that kept him from pursuing his artistic talent began to subside. He felt his body relax and a new drive to pursue his art.

Reflecting on my own humble meditation practice, it took me about five years of ongoing training until I finally presented my teacher at the time with the earth-shattering insight of what it was that was going on in my head every day: "It's all about me!" He just smiled and nodded, conveying the message that he'd heard it a thousand times before, for one simple reason: because it is so stunningly and essentially *human*. We are all inherently self preoccupied. Even if we put our needs second and let others shine in daily life, the chatter in our heads is almost exclusively a jumbled mess about our worries, and how we come across, and what we have to do, and why we were treated this way and on and on and on. We have to be honest about who and where we are in our development. Pretending to be selfless gets us nowhere — and usually simply serves the purpose of making us feel superior to the "poor schmucks" who don't seem to have a grasp of themselves. It's the same thing with giving up on our own needs and always putting everybody else first. Before we can lose ourselves, we have to find ourselves. Nobody can give something that isn't there in the first place. Not even the self.

Nature and Healing

Sometimes other people are too much to take. When we feel vulnerable and don't have an ally nearby, the connection with nature may be just as meaningful as the one with people. Nature is a part of our lives. We, as urban creatures, tend to neglect nature's contribution to our well-being and its role in the circle of life. Nature in itself can be soothing because there are no people against whom we have to compete. While in reality animals chase each other in the hunt for survival, and plants grow and die in front of our eyes, most of us humans don't feel threatened when we are in the woods or by the ocean. We experience the absence of others as peaceful, and feel connected to the beings around us. The British writer Neil Ansell described this journey in his book *Deep Country*. He had retreated from life into a log cabin in the English countryside for five years, away from people, living off the land:

"What I found was not what you might expect. You might think that such protracted solitude would lead to introspection, to self-examination, to a growing self-awareness. But not for me. What happened to me was that I began to forget myself, my focus shifted almost entirely outwards to the natural world outside my window. It was as if we gain our sense of self from our interaction with other people; from the reflection of ourselves we see in the eyes of another. Alone, there was no need for identity, for self-definition. I disappeared from my own story."

Growing Up

A little while ago, I got a phone call from the people who do the Gallup surveys. At first, I wasn't crazy about having to give up time for this unsolicited request, but afterwards I was glad I had participated. They were asking random people about their happiness. The pollster asked questions like the following: Did I laugh at least once on the previous day? Do I have people I can confide in? Am I comfortable with my income? Do I belong to a religious group? Did I feel sad the previous day? Did I experience physical pain? Did I worry a lot? Do I have a chronic illness? We ran down the questionnaire pretty quickly. The previous day, which served as a measuring tool, wasn't the best day I'd ever had. I was in an ongoing quarrel with a colleague who was important to me, and the sadness and conflict I felt about it came out in my answers. But looking at the big picture, I realized that there was nothing wrong with my life. Yes, I was a hung up on an argument I had with another therapist. No, I don't live the perfect life. But all in all, I have it pretty good. Once we sort through our childhood trauma and the many disappointments we've had to go through in our life, we can afford to try to find *gratitude* for what we have and make it an ongoing practice to be appreciative each day.

The path to an emotionally fulfilled life is the "middle way," the way of negotiation and compromise. Growing up means not just stopping to buy into the crazy loops our minds tend to spin. It also means giving up our self-centered point of view and negotiating with the people around us, to biting the bullet and giving in a little. It's all about balance. Some of us give in too easily. Others too little. We need to find the middle way in order to be happy. We must learn to gauge what is too important for us to surrender, and when we can join the other in their perspective. For someone who always gives in, it's a good sign when a kernel of competitiveness kicks in, when you don't just automatically back down but start to hold your own ground. When feelings of jealousy and unfairness come up, it means not having to resort to pleasing again as the only way of coping. If we can insist on having our way one time, it's not as difficult to let go on another occasion.

It's easy to get hung up on the stressors of daily life, on our anxieties and worries. Of course there are very legitimate obstacles that prevent us from being happy. But all too often we get caught up in tunnel vision. We focus on our negative self-image, our fears of being inadequate or being unable to live up to other people's expectations. It's the hardest thing to just *accept ourselves* the way we are. So what if we feel awkward sometimes when meeting new people? So what that our minds immediately race towards the worst case scenario? Well, that's what the mind does. Let it do its thing. It doesn't have to stop us from enjoying our lives.

Leave yourself alone. Wear out those voices in your head that are constantly critical of yourself. If you can accept yourself, you can accept others. We can start to forgive our families and friends for their foolishness when it feels right, because we know that we can be as foolish at times. The stronger we get, the less threatened we feel by their idiosyncrasies.

Stay engaged with the people in your life. Stay engaged with the world. Don't let your impulse to retreat from life take over. Take on the attitude of the warrior. Face the challenges life throws at you. And if it gets too much, allow yourself to take a break. It's all about the middle way.

Take care of somebody else. Have or mentor a child. Get a dog. Grow some flowers. Volunteer. Take care of your sick sister. Sometimes we forget that we are just as important to others as they are to us. You too have something to give. There is always someone who wants what you have to offer. And if they want too much, give yourself a break. Remember the middle way.

Wisdom, as the ancient Greeks used to say, is coming to terms with your own limitations. Just don´t buy into your fear that all you have *is* limitations.

6. The Costs of Individualism — An Immigrant Experience

When I first arrived in the United States I was very taken with the American culture, which communicated a great deal of openness and tolerance to me. As a German citizen I grew up with a certain plainness and a perpetual social scrutiny in daily conduct, which was so fittingly described in an article by the venerable German newspaper *Süddeutsche Zeitung*. The paper printed a review of the American satire *Asshole: How I Got Rich and Happy by Not Giving a Damn About Anyone.* The book tells the story of the attempted transformation of a self-described notorious pleaser who wanted to become a strong and powerful macho man by turning into, well, an asshole. According to asshole etiquette, being successful in this endeavor comes with certain conditions, and the paper quotes: "Think: How does an asshole walk down the street? First thing is he goes where he wants and doesn't pay too much attention to trivia like WALK signs, ambulances and other human beings. If you want to stop, you stop without looking behind yourself first. If you happen to bump into someone there are wild accusations hurled at the victim, and a swiftly hoisted middle finger." Upon which the paper comments: "At this point we wonder what kind of self-help book this is, which sounds like it is describing the everyday social conduct in Berlin."

In fact, after 33 years of being fed a diet of *respect the authorities – and if you don't, make sure nobody catches you*, alternating with *I will ignore that SOB next to me who is only out to get my subway seat, the last bratwurst from the grill, my girlfriend, or – worst of all – blocks the passing lane on the autobahn with his lame-ass hybrid vehicle*, I experienced the American way of being with each other not just as refreshingly casual but also as generous and inclusive. A friendly *Have a nice day!* sounded to me like angels singing, and the habitual *You're welcome* became an ongoing invitation to hang around, heralding understanding and acceptance. I experienced the general style of communication in the U.S. as a lot more engaging, and I loved the ease with which seeming strangers approach each other at a party or other social gatherings. Where introverted people in Germany stand around alone, waiting to grow mold until someone approaches them, in America everybody seems to be welcomed with open arms and is easily included in any conversation.

But every coin has two sides, and social mores are no different. Even though it often takes far more for a German to overcome initial awkwardness and alienation, once you become friends you can be pretty sure of a lasting relationship. In Germany, new friends will call each other and make an effort to go to readings and the movies together or just sit in a beer garden and yap the evening away. If one of you moves to a different city, the travel-eager and often childless German will include you in his holiday planning and pay frequent visits. It's not quite as simple in the U.S., or at least in New York City.

Lots of newcomers are certainly excited to work or study in a big city like New York and are open to making friends from any class or ethnicity. They often gain a more or less large circle of friends quickly and enjoy the excitement of building a brand new life. But there are obstacles. American employers don't necessarily accept the training or professional experience immigrants have gained in their home country. There are countless tales of Russian engineers, German advertising professionals and Indian teachers who have to work for a minimum wage at McDonald's or can't work at all because they lack professional experience in the U.S. or because of certain visa restrictions. The hunt for a job and the necessity to make money weighs heavily on their minds, and there is no time or energy to look for those vital social connections.

The job market isn't the only problem. Many people also feel increasingly isolated. Without having a place to go to work every day, the social environment that automatically comes with having a job is lacking. In some cultures, especially in Europe, many couples don't have children and find themselves unable to connect with any of the families in their new suburban American neighborhood, who are often mostly interested in family life and joint activities with other children. At the same time, European ethnicities, whose peak immigration waves took place in the 1800s, no longer form the typical enclaves that new immigrants from Latin America or East and Southeast Asia find already established. People from all over the world come to the U.S. without having any family or community waiting for them and literally have to make it on their own. "Even though it is easy to meet people in the grocery store or at a party, I find it extremely hard to build an actual relationship with other American women," someone once complained to me. "They always seem to be too busy to squeeze time out of their overloaded schedules to just hang out with a girlfriend."

Many expatriates and new immigrants find themselves struggling to find like-minded friends who are willing to take a Sunday afternoon to sit in a coffee house and just talk, instead of being squeezed into their lunch break on a workday. Often they've left behind a large circle of friends and colleagues in their hometown with a regular job and fixed working hours. In many societies the pace of life is much slower, and simply taking it easy and hanging out is just as good an activity as going to a ball game or to the theater, which Americans prefer. Many immigrants are not used to the American way of needing to work endless hours of overtime to make ends meet and prefer to go home at night to their families. Sometimes these differences are palpable even between the regions in the U.S., so that a Midwesterner might find himself alienated by the constant and competitive "rat race" in a place like New York City.

The overall mobility in the U.S. contributes to this trend. Because of lower wages, unstable social benefits and the constant competitive pressure at the workplace, many American workers don't feel the same loyalty to their employers that many Europeans or Asians do. They prefer a job that pays better but is located on the other side of the country, and seem to adjust their families to a brand new life and a new social environment easily. People who are left behind—especially those who recently immigrated and are still finding their way through a new system—experience a vague sense of loneliness and disruption: The fragile friendships that were established are lost when those new-found friends move away. And because many immigrants make friends with other immigrants who may then decide to go back to their home country, these connections fall apart as well.

Hence, part of the dynamic that immigrants, and not only immigrants, are struggling with is the great mobility of Americans as well as their inherent cultural ideal of individualism, as opposed to the more community-oriented organization of European, African, Asian, or South American societies. The often quoted historian and social commentator Alexis de Tocqueville wrote in his 1835 study titled *Democracy in America* how individualism brings with it "a calm and considered feeling which disposes each citizen to isolate himself from the mass of his fellows and withdraw into the circle of family and friends."

While Germans and other nationalities form much of their social life around associations and communities—nowhere more typical than in the sports club—Americans organize their lives according to the principles of individualism and independence: they prefer going to the gym alone when they can fit it into their schedule rather than joining a volleyball team that plays at a certain time. They go to the movies or get a DVD to watch on their own time rather than organizing a card game that has to accommodate several players. They prefer an online course that provides flexibility to a classroom at a location that they have to stand in traffic for a couple of hours to get to. The trend of the superiority of self-determination and personal freedom was impressively described in Robert Putnam's groundbreaking study *Bowling Alone*, in which he observed — among many other things — more and more Americans going to the bowling alley by themselves rather than playing on an organized sports team, which he saw as a symptom of the weakening community life and increasing social isolation of many Americans.

Putnam describes how the decline of communal activities began in the second half of the last century. According to his analysis, the most important reasons are the daily pressures of not having enough time and having to make money, as well as the development of urban sprawl, which adds more time to the daily commute to and from work. But the ubiquitous presence of technology and the mass media also takes a big slice of time out of the day that used to be available for friends and community. Of course, making friends online counts as social activity too, but again, the distance and the boundaries between online buddies and the friends on your sports team are on average far greater, not to mention the overall separating qualities of email and text messaging.

According to Putnam, the predominant factor in this development is a generational shift. Baby boomers, the generation born roughly between 1946 and 1964, tended to distance themselves from their more conformist parents, who grew up with the traditional matrix of father the provider and mother the housekeeper, who had two kids and a car and a house together. Baby boomers wanted more from life, started to rebel, and preferred values like individualism, tolerance for other races and self-actualization. They were and still are skeptical of authority and most forms of organized religion or even political activism, and they identify themselves more as individuals than as members of a group.

The same goes for the generation following the boomers, the so-called Generation X, whose members were born roughly between 1965 and 1980. They have been described as the "lost generation," which grew up with skyrocketing divorce rates, the demise of the traditional family, the absence of unifying political figures, the arms race of the 1980s, and coming of age under uncertain economic conditions. Because there were few public or cultural role models and plenty of personal insecurities to deal with, they often turned inward and toward an even greater individualism and more materialistic goals. *Time* magazine stated in 1987: "They are an unsung generation, hardly recognized as a social force or even noticed much at all. . . . They feel influenced and changed by the social problems they see as their inheritance: racial strife, homelessness, AIDS, fractured families and federal deficit.".

Putnam points out that, in addition, a change in mood took place at the end of the last century. The younger population groups reported a lot more emotional distress, depression, insomnia, even suicide than the previous generations. This too seems to be one of the consequences of greater social isolation and alienation from a larger community life, and the rampant individualism of these times leads to depression a lot quicker when there's also a lack of community.

The present generation, called the Millennials and they were born after 1980, grapple with their own issues. Because of the influence of Internet and mobile technologies, they are mostly seen as a lot more inclusive, communicative, socially responsible, used to diversity, and as valuing progressive politics. They are not rebelling against the existing institutions or big business but seeking transformation toward a greater public good by working within these organizations. At the same time, because they have been raised by their parents to expect things to revolve around them, they have a generally lower frustration tolerance and often have a hard time keeping their demands at bay. According to *60 Minutes,* "They need pampering, some say coddling, and if you don't tell them what they want to hear, they are gone."

Individualism and narcissism often go hand in hand. In a strong community, generally only a few leaders get to shine, and hopefully not at the expense of its members. In an individualistic society, the lonely winner, the outstanding hero, the rugged cowboy who rides off into the sunset alone after saving the world from evil are all admired. Community life rarely has the necessary sex appeal to be featured in a good news story or a Hollywood movie. If it is, it will be portrayed as a group of last-century Luddites as in M. Night Shyamalan's *The Village* or as a band of soldiers or firefighters. Appearing in the most successful movies are figures like Superman, James Bond and Indiana Jones, who shoulder the burden of doing good all by themselves; Wild West heroes played by John Wayne; and headstrong and powerful characters like Citizen Kane, Lawrence of Arabia, and the Godfather. Many executives name books by Ayn Rand, the 20th-century Russian immigrant who greatly idealized individualism over the oppressive forms of socialism, as favorites. Her novels portray strong-willed loners who despise conformists and organized community life as a place where the masses are manipulated and disowned, and where lonely and ruthless individuals are the ones who ultimately succeed.

In a comical yet telling way, this is what Martin Kihn was after when he tried to convert himself into an "asshole." Tired of being pushed around and seemingly outperformed by an obnoxious colleague, he tried to deny his innately compromising and inclusive nature and headed out to toughen himself up. He even hired a coach who told him to cut lines and get beat up in a boxing ring in order to rehearse being a real-life ass. Two of Kihn's "secrets of asshole body language" include "Above all, do NOT 'mirror' what other people do" as a warning, because doing so "builds rapport," as well as "Always lead with your crotch, even if your pants are on." Kihn eventually got a better job and made more money, not because he had acquired some temporary bad habits but because he worked harder and therefore did a better job than his "Nemesis," who eventually self-destructed in the midst of his rampant "assholeness." All his plotting, manipulation and competitiveness, excluding colleagues and the larger work community, got the Nemesis nowhere and opened the doors for the seemingly weaker yet compromising opponent.

The psychologist Robert Karen traces the larger development of societies back to the Industrial Revolution. Even though pre-industrial societies were hierarchical, scarce in personal freedom and back-breakingly difficult, they did provide people with a strong sense of belonging. Everyone had parents and siblings to go home to, relatives and an extended family to socialize with, and a community — often related to class — that experienced the same kind of hardships, or progress, for that matter. People didn't move anywhere. They spent their lives on the same farm, in the same town and the same neighborhood. Karen writes:

The Industrial Revolution and the shift in customs and ethics that went along with it caused the world to gradually change from one in which people were born into a God-given place, with clearly ordered rules and duties, to one in which they had to make their place. Competition became a new organizing principle, and in one sphere after another it was becoming impossible to feel quite the same unity with one's fellows. Dependency, an unnecessary concept before, became an undesirable quality in men and, much later, in women. Meanwhile, as old bonds dissolved or became less central to one's life, the sphere of intimacy that surrounded each person shrank.

With the compulsion to prove yourself came the desire for perfection and achievement, as well as the necessity to spend more time at work and less time at home, with neighbors or by yourself, which could be used to create trust, intimacy or simply an opportunity to contemplate one's life. Idleness and passivity became something despicable and equivalent to laziness. Instead, productivity turned into the predominant criteria with which to measure a person's worth. Families were torn apart by the increased mobility, and young mothers, who used to have sisters, cousins, and aunts around them all day, were left alone with their children. Thus mother became the only person who provided for all of her child's needs, and if she failed, the baby was doomed. It was around this time that Freud discovered the first neuroses in young women, who were tormented by self-doubt and a failure to make intimate connections.

The trend continues today. "The Lonely American Just Got a Bit Lonelier" read a recent *New York Times* headline about a study by sociologists at the University of Arizona and Duke University. They found that most Americans have only two people to talk to about their private lives, and a quarter of the survey participants had no one at all. Chronically overworked and under financial pressure, with little energy left to socialize outside the immediate family, many Americans disengage from public life — although they thoroughly miss it.

New immigrants to the U.S. feel the pain, too. Many of them struggle with visa problems, institutional differences, insufficient health care and communication problems, and they are sometimes forced to take menial jobs far below their educational qualifications and have to give up their previous economic and social lifestyle. "It is assumed that depressive states are almost inevitably part of the migrant's adjustment during resettlement and acculturation," states the Canadian psychiatrist Granville da Costa in a study entitled *Depression Among Immigrants and Refugees.* "The reality is that depression may be evident not at the time of immigration, but only some years down the road."

Social isolation breeds emotional pain. According to the World Mental Health Survey, Americans top the worldwide scale of anxiety disorders. Forty million Americans suffer from unusually high anxiety, and it is the result of the high stress levels and a certain disconnect between the individual and a larger social network that could provide support and comfort.

Although the mental health issues of immigrants are slowly coming into public awareness in the U.S., most centers for immigrants have to focus on the more pressing needs of poorer migrants from Central America, Africa and Asia, for example, who also need help navigating the new culture. Because of our mutual cultural heritage, Europeans and Australians especially are often expected to adjust well and assimilate quicker than other populations. But that doesn't mean that they don't suffer from similar psychological pressures. "Stress and cultural issues affect upper-income levels too," says Ricarda Dowling, director of Communications at the Center for Multicultural Services. "Getting help for mental health issues still carries a certain stigma and shame in many communities."

Looking at my own history and why I came to the U.S., I wonder just how many immigrants, consciously or unconsciously, not only come in the hope of something better but also because they needed to leave something behind they felt unable to cope with — something that seemed worse than dealing with the complications of reassembling one's whole life. So many people come because of war, genocide, economic hardship, and dysfunctional families. These immigrants needed to get away from something, felt threatened by something, needed space and peace and room to breathe — away from those who hurt them. If the U.S. is a nation of immigrants who needed to withdraw from something, has it become a nation of withdrawers too? Do the children and grandchildren of immigrants deal with some remnants of trauma and, like their ancestors, learn to deal with their own traumas in the same way? Maybe the big melting pot is not just a place to fulfill our dreams and pursue our goals, but also a resting place to heal our wounds.

Bibliography

American Film Institute. *America's 10 Greatest Films in 10 Classic Genres*. AFI.com/10top10.

Ansell, N. (2011, March 27). My Life as a Hermit. *The Guardian*.

Beebe, Beatrice (2005). Mother-Infant Research Informs Mother-Infant Treatment. *Psychoanalytic Study of the Child, 60*, 6-46

Berzoff J., Flanagan L. M. & Hertz, P. (2002). *Inside Out and Outside In. Psychodynamic Clinical Theory and Practice in Contemporary Multicultural Contexts*. Lanham: Rowman & Littlefield.

Blakeslee, S. (2006, January 20). Cells That Read Minds. *The New York Times*.

Cacioppo, J. T. & Patrick, B. (2008). *Loneliness: Human Nature and the Need for Social Connection*. New York: W. W. Norton & Company.

Clark, T. (2011). *Nerve*. New York: Little, Brown and Company.

da Costa, G. (1993). Depression among immigrants and refugees. In P. Cappeliez & R. J. Flynn (Eds.), *Depression and the Social Environment*. Montreal: McGill-Queen's Press.

de Tocqueville, A. (2003). *Democracy in America*. New York: Penguin Classics.

Demott, J. S. (1987, February 23). Welcome, America, to the Baby Bust. *Time Magazine.*

Dowling, S. (1985). The Narcissistic Pursuit of Perfection. *Journal of the American Psychoanalytic Association, 33(S)*, 256-261.

Dumm, T. (2008). *Loneliness as a Way of Life.* Cambridge: Harvard University Press.

Election Special. (2008, November 17). *Newsweek.*

Fairbairn, W. R. (1952). *An Object-Relations Theory of the Personality: Schizoid Factors in the Personality.* London: Routledge & Kegan Paul.

Fountain, H. (2006, July 2). The Lonely American Just Got a Bit Lonelier. *The New York Times.*

Fromm-Reichmann, F. (1990). Loneliness. *Contemporary Psychoanalysis, 26,* 305-329.

Gendlin, E. T. (1968). The Experiential Response. In: E. Hammer (Ed.). *Use of Interpretation in Treatment.* New York: Grune & Stratton.

Guntrip, H. (1968). *Schizoid Phenomena, Object Relations and the Self.* London: Hogarth Press.

Harris, S. (2006, March 22). A Phenomenological Investigation of the Experience of Ambivalence. *Journal of Phenomenological Psychology.*

Interview with Nicholas Chistakis. (2008, July 14). Der Spiegel, pp. 138-40.

Johnson, S. M. (1994). *Character Styles.* New York: W.W. Norton & Company.

Karen, R. (1994). *Becoming Attached. First Relationships and How They Shape our Capacity to Love.* Oxford: Oxford University Press.

Kiersky S. & Beebe, B. (1994). The Reconstruction of Early Nonverbal Relatedness in the Treatment of Difficult Patients. *Psychoanalytic Dialogues,* 4(3), 389-408.

Kihn M. (2008). *Asshole. How I Got Rich and Happy by Not Giving a Damn About Anyone & How You Can, Too.* New York: Broadway Books.

Kohut, H. (1977). *The Restoration of the Self.* New York: International Universities Press.

_____ (1984). *How Does Analysis Cure?* Chicago: University of Chicago Press.

_____ & Wolf, E. (1978). The Disorders of the Self and their Treatment: An Outline. *International Journal of Psychoanalysis,* 59:413-425.

_____ (1968). The Psychoanalytic Treatment of Narcissistic Personality Disorders. *Psychoanalytic Study of the Child, 23,* 86-113.

Lee, R. & Martin, J. C. (1991). *Psychotherapy after Kohut. A Textbook of Self Psychology.* Hillsdale: The Analytic Press.

Lessem, P. A. (2005). *Self Psychology. An Introduction.* Lanham: Rowman & Littlefield.

Magid, B. (2001). *Ordinary Mind. Exploring the Common Ground of Zen and Psychotherapy.* Somerville, MA: Wisdom.

_____ (2008). *Ending the Pursuit of Happiness.* Somerville, MA: Wisdom.

Mayer, V. (2008, June 15). Sex and the City on Testosterone. *Süddeutsche Zeitung.*

McPherson, M., Smith-Lovin, L. & Brashears, M. Social isolation in America: Changes in Core Discussion Networks over Two Decades. *American Sociological Review, 71*(3), 353-375.

McWilliams, N. (1994). *Psychoanalytic Diagnosis.* New York: The Guilford Press.

Mendelson, M.D. (1990). Reflections on Loneliness. *Contemporary Psychoanalysis, 26,* 330-355.

Mijuskovic, B. (1979-80). Loneliness and Narcissism. *Psychoanalytic Review 66,* 479-492.

Mirror, Mirror in the Brain: Mirror Neurons, Self-understanding and Autism Research. (2007, November 7). *Science Daily.*

Morley, W. & Hais, M.D. (2008). *Millennial Makeover.* Piscataway: Rutgers University Press.

Putnam, R. D. (2000). *Bowling Alone. The Collapse and Revival of American Community.* New York: Simon & Schuster.

Rothstein, A. (1991). On Some Relationships of Fantasies of Perfection to the Calamities of Childhood. *International Journal of Psycho-Analysis, 72*, 313-323.

Safer, Morley. (2007, November 11). *Millennials*. November 11, 2007. CBS.com.

Slavin M. O. & Kriegman, D. (1998). Why the Analyst Needs to Change. *Psychoanalytic Dialogues, 8*(2), 247-284.

Stolorow, R., Brandchaft, B. & Atwood, G. (1988). *Psychoanalytic Treatment: An Intersubjective Approach.* Hillsdale, NJ: The Analytic Press.

Tillich, P. (1952). *The Courage to Be.* New Haven: Yale University Press.

Tilly, C. (2008). *Credit and Blame.* Princeton: Princeton University Press

Tronick, E. Z. (1989) Emotions and Emotional Communication in Infants. *American Psychologis,. 44*(2), 112-19.

Winerman, L. (2005, October). The Mind's Mirror. *Monitor on Psychology*.

Winnicott, D. (1965). Ego Distortion in Terms of True and False Self. In *The Maturational Process and the Facilitating Environment: Studies in the Theory of Emotional Development* (pp. 140-152). New York: International UP Inc.

Wolf, E. (1988). Treating the Self. Elements of
Clinical Self Psychology. New York: Guilford Press.

About the Author:

Gerti Schoen started her career as a journalist in Germany, which brought her to the United States as a foreign correspondent. Inspired by the dynamic energy of New York City, she decided to change careers and became a psychotherapist and at the same time a Zen practitioner. She lives with her husband and her two cats in the New York metropolitan area.

Made in the USA
Lexington, KY
21 May 2012